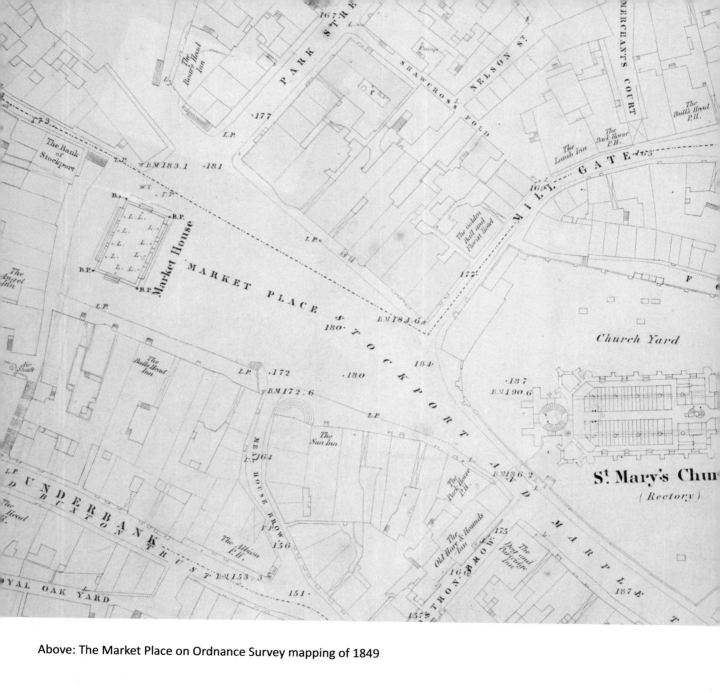

Above: The Market Place on Ordnance Survey mapping of 1849

From

Castle to Covered Market

A History of
Stockport's Market Place

Peter Arrowsmith

STOCKPORT
METROPOLITAN BOROUGH COUNCIL

Published by
Stockport Metropolitan Borough Council
2010

ISBN No 978-0-9553434-1-4

Printed on environmentally friendly paper by
Omega Print & Design
of Stockport

Back cover: A stone grotesque head on the chancel of St Mary's Church (Stockport MBC)

Contents

Acknowledgements

In 1996-7 I had the privilege to write, on behalf of Stockport Metropolitan Borough Council, the first detailed history of Stockport for over a century. This year it has also been my privilege to be invited to write a history of the town's Market Place and market, as part of the 750th celebrations of the granting of Stockport's market charter in 1260. I would like to thank Peter Ashworth, Head of Service: Culture, Tourism and Venues, for commissioning this book and Frank Galvin, Team Manager: Museums and Collections, for guiding it through to completion. Terry Mullaney, Senior Design Technician, Curatorial Service and Projects, has been invaluable in laying out the book as well as taking many of the photographs and I thank him for his hard work and dedication. Thanks are also due to Margaret Myerscough, Senior Librarian, Heritage and Archives, and the staff of Stockport Local Heritage Library for their continuous assistance; to Joanne Dunn, Collections Access Officer, Social History, for providing access to material in the Stockport Story Museum, and for her comments on a draft of the book; and to Katie Cavanagh, Collections Officer, and Angela Nesic, Collections Assistant, for locating material in the Stockport Museums Collections.

This book would have been the poorer without the assistance of the other curators, archivists, and librarians who retrieved material, provided images and gave permission for publication. For this, thank are due to Norman Redhead, County Archaeologist, and the staff of the Greater Manchester Archaeological Unit; Jonathan Pepler, Archivist, and the staff of the Cheshire Record Office; Richard Ovenden, Keeper of Special Collections and Associate Director, The Bodleian Libraries, University of Oxford; Dr Michael Powell, Librarian, and the staff of Chetham's Library, Manchester; Ros Westwood, Derbyshire Museums Manager; Lucy Yarham, House and Collections Manager, Sudbury Hall and the Museum of Childhood, The National Trust; and Janice Hayes, Principal Museum Manager, and Craig Sherwood, Documentation Access Officer, Warrington Central Library Museum and Art Gallery. Records in the Cheshire Record Office are reproduced with the permission of Cheshire Shared Services and the owner/depositor to whom copyright is reserved.

The painting of the Warren Family by George Romney is in a private collection; permission for its publication was kindly provided by the owner, and the assistance of Alex Kidson, Consultant Curator, National Museums Liverpool, in this matter is gratefully acknowledged. Julian Baum and Claire Duval of Take 27 Ltd, Chester, provided digital reconstructions of Staircase House. The photographs of the Market Place traders were taken by Pauline Neild. The Reverend Roger Scoones, Rector of St Mary's, Stockport, gave permission to photograph and reproduce material held at the church. Thanks are due to Hollie Fisher, Assistant Archivist, The Marks & Spencer Company Archive, for information on Ephraim Marks, and to Peter Crew for his expert opinion on the Shawcross Fold tile.

The present book was compiled in spring and early summer 2010 but a publication on the Market Place has long been an aspiration, and in this respect the continuing support and involvement of Paul Hartley, Team Manager: Conservation and Heritage, and Melissa Marshall, Project Officer, Stockport MBC, is gratefully acknowledged. Thank you also to the market traders and business proprietors of the Market Place. Finally I owe a special thank you to Adele, for her love, support and patience.

Peter Arrowsmith

Stockport, July 2010

List of Illustrations

Foreword

On the 6th September 1260 a market charter was granted to Robert de Stokeport III by Edward, Lord of Chester, the future King of England. At about the same date Stockport also received its borough charter. Together these two charters mark the beginning of the history of Stockport as a town.

To mark the 750th Anniversary of the granting of its market charter in 2010, Stockport Council has commissioned this new history of Stockport's Market Place.

This comprehensive and thoroughly researched account has been written by Dr Peter Arrowsmith who is an acknowledged expert on the history of Stockport. Dr Arrowsmith has uncovered many fascinating facts about the history of Stockport which he has woven into this compelling account, *From Castle to Covered Market: A History of Stockport's Market Place.*

The book draws extensively upon the town's Museum and Local Heritage Library collections. Many of the more important items connected with the history of the market can be seen in the Stockport Story Museum in the Market Place, where a specially commissioned audio-guide is also being made available for the first time to mark the 750th Anniversary of Stockport's market charter.

Stockport's market is held in great affection by Stockport people, who have always regarded it as being at the very heart of the town. It is appropriate that in this anniversary year the Market Place has never looked better, following extensive restoration and regeneration works to the historic fabric. But the prosperity of the market relies not just on bricks and mortar, or indeed cast iron and glass, but on the vitality brought by the people who live, work, shop and visit the market to enjoy all that it has to offer.

I hope this book will provide new insights into the colourful history of Stockport Market and through its pages readers will glimpse something of the character that has given it a special place in the history of the town and makes it an important part of a prosperous future.

Dave Goddard

Councillor Dave Goddard
Leader of Stockport Metropolitan Borough Council

1. Introduction

The Market Place lies at the heart of Stockport's story. People may have been gathering on this site to trade before the Norman Conquest. A century or so after the Conquest a castle and parish church were built here. On the 6th of September 1260 the Lord Edward, the future King Edward I, granted a market charter to Robert de Stokeport, the lord of the manor. At about the same date Stockport also received its borough charter, which effectively marks the beginning of its history as a town. The historic Market Place was the physical core around which the early town developed. Its role as Stockport's commercial centre continued even when the town massively expanded during the Industrial Revolution (1.1, 1.3). For a long time it was also Stockport's administrative hub, with the management of the market and town being carried out in a succession of buildings situated on and adjacent to the Market Place. It lay at the centre of daily life in the town and was the setting of many events in Stockport's history.[1]

The story of Stockport's Market Place is also one of continuity. Of the many early market centres in the North West, some were relatively short-lived. Other places have continued to hold a market or have revived the same, but have moved this away from its original site. Stockport has the rare distinction that its market is held in its ancient Market Place (1.2, 1.8-1.23). Indeed, within the modern county of Greater Manchester, Stockport alone can make this claim.

The Market Place is also distinguished by its historic buildings and archaeological remains, many of which have been recorded in recent years during the renovation and conservation of this historic town core. A striking feature of the Market Place area is the sequence of buildings erected by the local authorities at different times in the town's history, a significant number of which still survive.

The present book has three main themes. The first is concerned with the market and fairs, and how these developed from earliest times until the nineteenth century when their control passed from the lord of the manor to the Corporation. The second is the sequence of buildings erected in and around the Market Place in connection with the market and the running of the town, beginning with Stockport's earliest known town hall and culminating in its Victorian Covered

Facing page: 1.1 Aerial view of the Market Place, from the now demolished chimney of the Newbridge Lane power station, 1981

Market (1.4). Some are still familiar features of the town, others have been lost, while some grand schemes were short-lived or never executed. The third main theme is that of the buildings which have surrounded the Market Place through the ages, their uses, occupants and changing appearance (1.5-1.7). These include some of Stockport's most important sites and structures, ranging from the castle and church, to Staircase House, a rare survival of an early town house, and the curious Castle Mill. The book also briefly looks at the renovation and conservation of the Market Place following failed attempts in the twentieth century for its radical redevelopment.

Above: 1.2 Stockport market today. Facing page: 1.3 Market day, about the 1890s

Facing page. Above: 1.4 The Market Place and the Covered Market from Castle Yard
Below left: 1.5 Looking from St Mary's Church. Below right: 1.6 Staircase House and the Stockport Story Museum
Above: 1.7 Nos 3-8 Market Place and (right) the entrance to Mealhouse Brow
Following pages: 1.8-1.23 Market day today

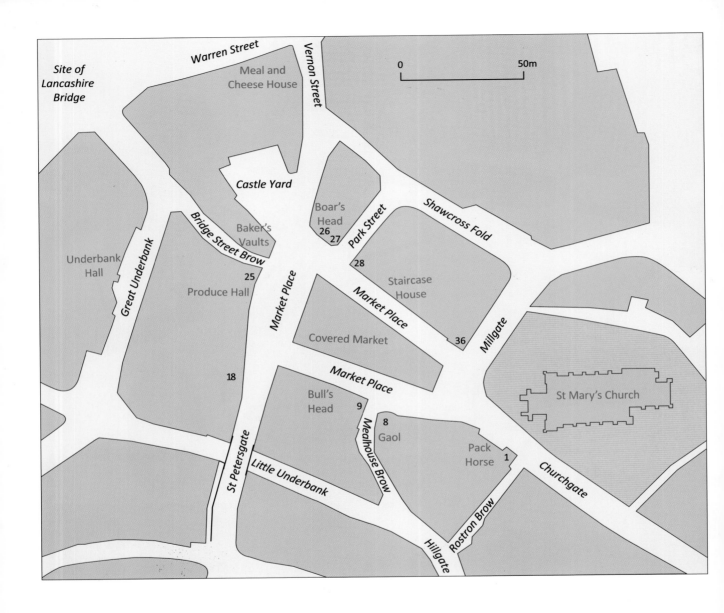

Above: 1.24 The Market Place and its surroundings

'Upon one round hill'

In the early nineteenth century it was said of Stockport that 'There is not in England a more irregular spot of ground than that on which this town stands'.[2] The Market Place itself occupies a promontory of land roughly triangular in shape (1.24). From here the ground falls away on the west to the River Mersey, on the north to the River Goyt, and on the south to a ravine cut by a tributary of the Mersey known as the Tin Brook. The brook is now culverted and the ravine is more familiar today as the street known as Little Underbank. At the north-west corner of the Market Place is a further, smaller triangular promontory. Historically this has been known as Castle Hill or Castle Yard, after the town's medieval castle. The elevated position of the Market Place was once a dominant feature of the town (1.25). William Webb in the early seventeenth century wrote that 'Upon one round hill hath this town of Stockport been built, the summit, or top whereof, affords the market-place, and convenient room for the church, and for the parsonage, which are very fair ones'.[3]

Above: 1.25 'Upon one round hill', the approach to the Market Place from Bridge Street Brow

Castle Hill and much of the Market Place promontory are formed from the sandstone bedrock. On the west and south, above the Underbanks, the sides of the hill were once evident as sandstone cliffs but over the centuries these have been modified and hidden by the development of the town. Adjacent properties were extended by cutting these cliffs into a vertical face and additional storage space was created by hollowing out the rock.[4] The north side of the Market Place has a gentler slope which descends towards the Goyt. The easiest approach to the Market Place is from the east, the site of the parish church of St Mary.

Stockport developed at the junction of two important communication routes, one between the north and south, the other between the east and west. Historically, the town lay within Cheshire, with the River Mersey forming the boundary with Lancashire. Immediately below Castle Hill is the site of Lancashire Bridge, an ancient bridging point over the Mersey, from where a road led northwards to Manchester. A ford, upstream of this bridge, provided an earlier crossing point. To the east of the town, beyond the hill of Werneth Low, is the entrance to the pass of Longdendale, one of the main trans-Pennine routes into Yorkshire. In the opposite direction lie the Cheshire plain and the city and former port of Chester.

Above: 1.26 The Bronze Age burial urn from Portwood
Facing page. Above: 1.27 Roman coins from Mellor
Below: 1.28 The Bronze Age flint dagger from Mellor

Origins

Stockport's location on high ground above the Mersey and other local watercourses would have made it a suitable place for settlement in prehistory. No finds of prehistoric date are at present known from the town centre, but Bronze Age burials have been discovered not far to the east in Portwood (1.26).[5]
The principal prehistoric site in the Stockport region is at Mellor, on the fringe of the Pennine uplands, where recent excavations have revealed evidence of occupation extending over several thousand years (1.28).

It is believed that two Roman roads crossed at Stockport.[6]
One was the road from Manchester to Buxton. The other was an east-west route running from the Roman fort of Melandra, near the entrance of Longdendale; to the west of Stockport this seems to have continued through Cheadle and probably joined with the road between Manchester and Chester. A scatter of Roman coins in and around Cheadle village hints at a possible settlement there, and Roman material has also been discovered in the excavations at Mellor (1.27). A small number of Roman finds, including coins and pottery, have been discovered at Stockport itself, concentrated on the Market Place and in particular on Castle Hill. They suggest that there was a Roman site here of some description but its nature remains elusive.[7]

Above: 2.1 Stockport's medieval borough charter, a foundation stone of the market town

2. The Medieval Market Place, 1066-1500

The earliest evidence for a market at Stockport is engrained in the very name of the place.[1] Its meaning has long been a subject of debate, fuelled by the diversity of early spellings. However, the name is first documented in the twelfth century as 'Stokeport', derived from the Old English 'stoc' and 'port'. The second of these words means a market place. The first is now understood to refer to a minor settlement and is sometimes translated as a 'hamlet'. Hence Stockport was 'the market place at the hamlet'. Although we cannot be certain on this point, the name may indicate that there was already a market here before the Norman Conquest. This early market can be supposed to have served as a central meeting place to which people from other places came to trade, mostly in agricultural produce.

Stockport does not appear in the Domesday Book of 1086 although other local places, Cheadle, Bredbury and Bramhall, are included. Its absence is itself perhaps a sign of its status as a hamlet within a larger manor, which may have been one of those other places. By the late twelfth century the situation had radically changed. Stockport had not only become a manor in its own right but was also the site of a castle. By this date its lord probably also controlled a sizeable group of other manors, collectively known as a barony, making him one of the most important figures in Cheshire.

The castle seems to have been relatively short-lived but the creation of the barony elevated Stockport's importance. By the end of the twelfth century a parish church was also founded here. In the thirteenth century the next stage of Stockport's development, in which the baron played a key role, was the establishment of a market town. By the later medieval period it was among the more prosperous of Cheshire's small towns. Local tradesmen and craftsmen had been joined by wealthy textile merchants, with trading links eastwards to Yorkshire and westwards to Chester and Ireland. The town had a strong leather-working industry and an early textile industry which seems to have included dyeing as well as weaving. It was also wealthy enough to have its own medical practitioners and goldsmiths.[2]

Stockport Castle

The castle was in existence by 1173 when Geoffrey de Costentin, the lord of Stockport, held it against King Henry II in the large-scale rebellion of that year.[3] This is both the first and the last occasion on which it is mentioned by medieval sources as a working castle. The origins of the castle are not known for certain but it is likely that it was built for strategic reasons rather than simply to safeguard the lord and his household. It stood on the northern boundary of Cheshire, at the meeting place of two important communication routes into the county. Only a bow shot from its walls was the ford across the Mersey while to the east was the eastern entrance to the county via Longdendale. It is also possible that the earl of Chester, the overlord of the county, authorized the creation of the Stockport barony and the building of the castle at the same time, with the manors which made up the barony providing the manpower and other resources needed to construct and maintain the castle. As for the date of its construction, a plausible time is during the reign of King Stephen (1135-54). This was a period of unrest and civil war, in which the earl of Chester was a key player, and was also a time of intense castle building.

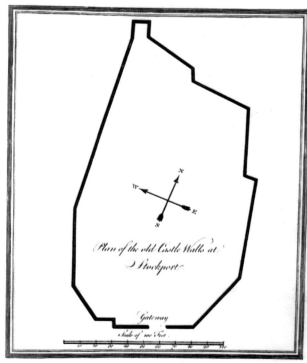

Precisely what role Stockport castle played in the revolt of 1173 is not recorded. Nor do we know its fate following the suppression of the rebellion. It is possible that Stockport was among the castles demolished on the order of the king. Alternatively this silence may simply reflect the infrequency with which castles in general, other than those of the king and the

Above: 2.2 The stone walls on Castle Hill, on the circa 1680 plan of the town
Below: 2.3 The 'old Castle Walls', the Reverend John Watson's plan of about 1775

18

most powerful lords, appear in the documentary record. With a few important exceptions, the majority of castles in the North-West seem to have gone out of use by the fourteenth century at the latest. That this was the case at Stockport may be suggested by a reference in 1336 to Castle Hill rather than to the castle itself.

Castle Hill was the early name of the triangular spur which projects from the north-west corner of the Market Place promontory, now flanked by Vernon Street and Bridge Street Brow. In the late seventeenth century a circuit of stone walls stood here, with a gateway onto the Market Place. They remained standing until the 1770s and enclosed an area known as Castle Yard, a name still used for this site.[4] The walls are depicted in a roughly circular form on the earliest plan of the town believed to date from about 1680 (2.2). In about 1775, shortly before their demolition, the Reverend John Watson, rector of Stockport, produced a plan of the 'old Castle Walls' (2.3). He claimed this to be based on accurate measurements and it does roughly correspond with a depiction of Castle Yard on a 1770 map of the town (4.1).[5] Watson's plan shows an irregular and angular circuit, some 30m by 60m, with a gateway onto the Market Place and, opposite this, a square projection suggestive of a small tower or possible postern (side) gate. The wall is shown with no significant thickness but may only be drawn as an outline.

Watson's plan was later used as the basis of fanciful reconstructions of a stone-built castle perched on the Castle Hill promontory and ringed with towers. More recently it has been supposed that the castle was of the motte and bailey type, with a motte or mound on Castle Hill surmounted by a keep, and a bailey or courtyard occupying the Market Place, and that this castle was originally built with timber walls which were later replaced in stone.[6]

The reality is that the form of the medieval castle is uncertain. Watson's plan might possibly show the curtain wall of a castle of the twelfth century. Although stone-built castles of this period were in the minority, one local example has been revealed by recent excavations at Buckton Castle near Stalybridge (2.4). Another possibility is that Watson's circuit represents the

Above: 2.4 Buckton Castle, the recently excavated castle wall

perimeter wall of a later medieval manor house built on the castle site. In about 1540 the antiquarian John Leland wrote that the lord of the manor, Edward Warren, was living at Poynton because 'Stoppord maner place is decayid', and his words suggest a site which was more obviously domestic than military in nature.[7] One element of the walls seems to be later still. The entrance to Castle Yard was described in 1775 as being closed by a door fastened to gateposts.[8] Gateposts are also shown here on the circa 1680 plan of the town and are depicted with ball finials, sug-

gestive of a seventeenth-century date. In 1685 the lord of the manor is reported to have recently built a stone wall on Castle Hill which encroached on the back of a neighbouring house, but this may have served as a revetment against the side of the hill rather than as part of the circuit on its summit.[9] The antiquarian William Stukeley in 1751 recorded that a Roman coin sent to him by an excise officer had been found 'on removal of some rubbish, called the Castle, at Stockport'.[10] The reference may be to some clearance of the area within the stone wall in the mid eighteenth century.

In 2003 archaeological investigations were carried out on Castle Hill during groundworks ahead of the new Courts development. These found no evidence of stone walls surviving in situ, and while a number of sandstone masonry blocks were exposed within the walls of later buildings they were of indeterminate date. The investigations did, how-ever, find one significant medieval feature, a well cut through the sandstone bedrock (2.5, 2.6). This was nearly 3m in diameter and survived to almost 6m in depth. Its backfill contained a number of cobbles, animal bones and two fragments of pottery dating from the fourteenth or fifteenth century. The bones were mainly cattle and horse and, from their condition, may be evidence of the provision of meat to feed a pig or household dog.[11] The size of the well would be

Above: 2.5 The medieval well on Castle Hill before excavation
Below: 2.6 Excavating the well

fitting for the castle, while its backfilling in the late medieval period reflects the decline of this once important site.

The Market Place Walls

While the early walls around Castle Yard have been lost, there are remains of sandstone walls below the south and west sides of the Market Place, hidden by buildings on Mealhouse Brow and Great Underbank (2.7, 2.8). These have been variously interpreted as town walls or as part of the castle.[12] However, town walls were rare in the North-West, with Chester being the only known instance in Cheshire, and it is highly improbable that Stockport was ever provided with such defences. The theory that the Market Place was once part of the castle dates back to the 1970s when archaeological investigations were carried out to the rear of property on the Market Place's north side. They revealed evidence of medieval activity but not the deep build-up

of material which was being discovered at the time in some medieval towns and cities. Since that date, however, excavations on other small medieval towns in the North-West have shown such shallow deposits to be the norm. Nor do the surviving lengths of wall below the Market Place appear defensive. They are situated against the sandstone cliffs, not on top of them, and seem to be retaining walls, designed to prevent the soft sandstone from eroding onto the properties below. The same fragments of stone wall have been patched with brick repairs, showing that they fulfilled a continuing use. The stone walls might be medieval, but they could equally well have been built at a later date, and we have already seen that a possible stone revetment wall was

Above: 2.7 The 'town wall' at Mealhouse Brow
Left: 2.8 The 'town wall' at Great Underbank

21

'Edward, the eldest son of the illustrious King of England, to his Archbishops, Bishops, Abbots, Priors, Earls, Barons, Justices, Sheriffs, Mayors, Ministers, and to all his Bailiffs and Faithful Men, greetings.
Know that we have granted to our beloved and faithful Robert de Stokeport that he and his heirs may have for ever one market at his manor of Stockport in our county of Chester on Thursday each week.
And that likewise they may have one fair in each year to last for eight days, that is, on St Wilfrid's day and for seven days following, unless that market and that fair are to the injury of neighbouring markets or neighbouring fairs. For which reason we wish and firmly instruct for ourselves and our heirs that the said Robert and his heirs may have for ever one market at his manor of Stockport in our county of Chester on Thursday each week. And that likewise they may have one fair in each year to last for eight days, that is, on St Wilfrid's day and for seven days following with all liberties and free customs belonging to the said market and fair, unless that market and that fair are to the injury of neighbouring markets or neighbouring fairs, as said. Given by our hand at Shotwick on the sixth day of September in the forty-fourth year of the reign of the Lord, the King, our Father.'

built against the side of Castle Hill in the late seventeenth century. The wall at Great Underbank includes a carved water-spout or gargoyle but this is suspected to have come from the old Stockport parish church demolished in 1810.[13] In the sixteenth and seventeenth centuries the name 'bastile' was associated with a plot of land in, or adjacent to, the Market Place containing houses and shops. At this date the term had the meaning of a 'tower' but the precise location of the 'Bastile Room or place' or 'Bastile houses' is at present unknown, and the name might derive from a feature of Castle Hill.[14] Even as revetments, the walls below the Market Place are of some interest, and highlight the problems imposed upon the development of the town's historic core by its natural topography.

Above: 2.9 The market charter, granted on the 6th of September 1260, copied in the late eighteenth century by the Reverend John Watson
Facing page: 2.10 A 1730 record of the market charter among the documents of the lord of the manor

The Market Charter and the Medieval Market

In the thirteenth century two documents provided the foundation stones of Stockport's future development. One of these was the borough charter. The other was the market charter, granted to Robert de Stokeport, the lord of the manor, on the 6th of September 1260. The grantor was the twenty-one year old Edward, the son of King Henry III, in his capacity as the Lord of Chester. The original charter has been lost but is known from a transcription made by the Reverend John Watson in the late eighteenth century, when the document was in the possession of the lords of the manor, the Warrens (2.9, 2.10).[15] The charter allowed a market to be held at Stockport every Thursday (the market was later moved to Friday) and a yearly fair to be held on eight days beginning on St Wilfrid's day. This feast day then fell on the 12th of October but following the amendment of the calendar in 1752 was moved to the 23rd.

The charter was not the beginning of a market in Stockport. The very name of the place is evidence of a market here at an earlier date but the charter put it on a firm legitimate footing. The granting of the charter reflects the conditions of the time. In the thirteenth century the population and the economy were expanding, and markets and fairs were on the rise. Both provided revenue for the local lords, who could charge a toll (a tax on goods sold) and stallage (a charge for the use of a market stall). Markets and fairs could be held simply by custom, but increasingly they were expected to have higher approval in the form of a charter, usually granted by the crown, for which the recipient paid a fee. The granting of such charters reached a peak in the third quarter of the thirteenth century, precisely the period to which the Stockport market charter belongs.[16]

Medieval weekly markets provided a place in which people could buy and sell foodstuffs, livestock and, to a lesser extent, manufactured goods. Annual fairs brought in traders from further afield. There are records of livestock being sold at Stockport in 1285, apples in 1358-9 and corn in 1518 when one unfortunate trader selling this produce, Ottiwell Booth, was stabbed to death in the Market Place.[17]

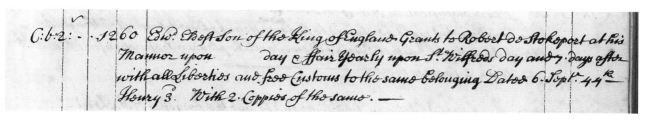

Although other annual fairs were added to Stockport's civic calendar, the St Wilfrid's fair was surrounded by the most ceremony. In the nineteenth century it was opened with an official proclamation in the Market Place.[18] The time of the fair was also when the town's mayor began the annual term of office.[19]

The market charter's clause that Stockport's market and fair should not be to the detriment of neighbouring markets and fairs was commonplace within such documents. At the time of the charter there were well-established markets and fairs at Macclesfield to the south, and Manchester and Salford to the north. Altrincham to the west and Glossop to the east were each given a charter in 1290.[20] In the 1280s traders from Stockport and Macclesfield seem to have operated in each other's market where, under the terms of their borough charters, the townspeople of both places should have been free from toll and stallage. In 1286 because of competition from Stockport's market and fair the town of Macclesfield was said to be 'sorely damaged'. Richard de Stokeport was forced to concede that he had wrongly charged traders from Macclesfield toll and stallage, but by producing the charter granted to his father in 1260 he was also able to ensure the continuation of his own market.[21]

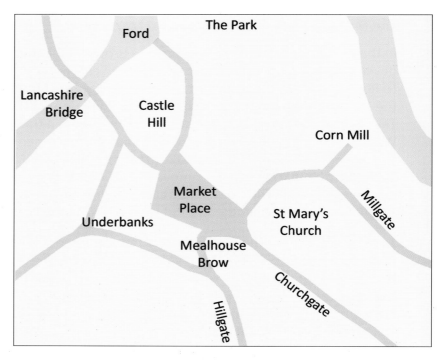

The Medieval Borough

By the late thirteenth century Stockport was not only a flourishing market centre but had also been elevated to a borough. This involved the creation of a class of burgesses, individuals who each possessed a plot of land known as a burgage. Burgages were primarily intended for housing and were in effect the building blocks of a town. The burgesses themselves enjoyed a

Above: 2.11 Streets of the medieval town

number of privileges in return for certain obligations to the lord of the manor, and these rights and dues were set out in the second of Stockport's key thirteenth-century documents, the borough charter.

The original borough charter has also been lost but a copy made in 1530 has survived and can be seen in the Stockport Story Museum (2.1).[22] In return for a burgage and a plot of land in Stockport's common fields, each burgess paid a rent of 1 shilling. The charter gave the burgesses of Stockport certain economic advantages. These included exemption from paying toll and stallage in the markets and fairs of Cheshire, with one exception; they were still liable for toll on the important commodity of salt bought at the three 'wichs', the salt-producing centres of Nantwich, Northwich and Middlewich. For their part, like other tenants of the manor, they were obliged to have their corn ground at the lord's mill 'should he have one'. Bread which was made for sale was to be baked in the lord's oven, with the same proviso.

The borough charter was granted by Robert de Stokeport and was based, according to its preamble, on a charter which he had received from the 'lord of Cheshire'. The charter is not dated and three Robert de Stokeports were lord of the manor in succession between the late twelfth century and the 1270s. In the nineteenth century it was supposed that the charter dated from about 1220. In 1904 Professor James Tait showed that the details of the charter over-whelmingly point to a later date, probably fairly close to the market charter of 1260.[23] Comparison with other local places which received borough charters in the thirteenth century also supports such a later date. Macclesfield, a more important place in medieval Cheshire than Stockport, was given its charter by the Lord Edward in 1261; this seems to have superseded an earlier charter given by the earl of Chester in about 1220-33. On the Lancashire side, Salford which was also an early place of importance, received its charter from the earl of Chester in about 1230. This document seems to have later been the model for the Stockport charter, and for the Bolton charter of 1253. Manchester's charter is dated 1301 but probably confirms and perhaps extends existing privileges. Indeed a date of about 1260 for the Stockport borough charter would still be relatively early compared with a number of other Cheshire towns (Congleton in 1272-4, Middlewich and Northwich both in 1288, Altrincham in about 1290, Knutsford in about 1292).[24]

The borough of Stockport may originally have contained about sixty burgages, although by the late fifteenth century the number had increased to ninety.[25] Many of the medieval burgages must have been located on the Market Place, the heart of the town. The present triangular plan of the Market Place probably dates back to the creation of the borough in the thirteenth century, with the street frontages of the surrounding properties following the line of the early burgages. It is also likely that many of the boundaries between those properties originated as the divisions between burgages. Medieval burgages were typically narrow elongated plots extending back from a roadway, but on the west and south sides of the Market Place the length of such plots was limited by the sandstone cliffs. Only the north side, with its gentler slope towards the River Goyt, was free from this constraint and it is possible that from the outset the burgages here were the most desirable.

As well as the Market Place, the medieval town included several streets (2.11). Millgate, Hillgate and Underbank (the street below the 'bank' or cliff) are all mentioned as the site of burgages in the fifteenth century, and Churchgate in 1541. Millgate, 'the road to the mill', took its name from one of Stockport's two manorial corn mills. The other, probably later, mill was in existence by the seventeenth century and was situated in the area below Castle Hill known as the Park.

Mealhouse Brow or, as it was known in the seventeenth century, Wynn Bank was probably also in existence in the medieval period and may have originated as a natural gully which provided access to the Market Place from Hillgate. By the seventeenth century the manorial bakehouse was situated at its foot. Bridge Street Brow and Vernon Street, situated to either side of Castle Hill, were also probably both medieval routeways. Vernon Street seems to have originally led down to the ancient ford across the Mersey. Bridge Street Brow gave access to the bridge over the river. Lancashire Bridge, as it came to be known, was in existence by the 1280s. It was rebuilt on several occasions, most notably in the eighteenth century after having been broken in an attempt to prevent the Jacobite army of Bonnie Prince Charlie from crossing the river here on its march south. In the medieval period this was one of

Above: 2.12 Staircase House, the curving blades of the medieval crucks

only three bridges along the entire course of the Mersey. For one late seventeenth-century commentator, the importance of Stockport could be summed up by reference to only two attributes, its bridge and its market. The construction of the first undoubtedly helped the success of the second.[26]

Staircase House

Remarkably, the remains of one medieval dwelling on the Market Place still survive within Staircase House.[27] It was built using timber crucks, or A-frames, as the main structural supports (2.12-2.14). Originally the building contained four crucks, of which the central two are partly extant (3.16). Recent archaeological investigations have also revealed the remains of a wall built of stone and tile, which carried the timber-framed outer wall of the building (2.15). The two end bays each seem to have been divided into an upper and lower floor but smoke blackening on the upper timbers may indicate that the central bay was open to the roof and was heated by a central hearth. It is likely that this room was a hall, the principal room in a medieval house, where meals would have been taken and visitors admitted. The date of the cruck-framed building is known from tree-ring dating samples taken from the western surviving cruck in 1988. These showed the timber to have been felled in the winter of 1459-60. Winter felling of trees was common, with building work beginning in the following spring.

There is good reason to believe that this cruck-framed building occupied the front of a burgage plot. In the

Above: 2.13 Staircase house, the apex of a medieval cruck
Below: 2.14 Artist's reconstruction of the cruck-framed Staircase House in 1460

mid seventeenth century the owners of Staircase House paid a chief rent of 1 shilling to the lord of the manor, the rent set for a burgage under the medieval borough charter. When the property was sold in 1738 it was explicitly described as 'all that ancient burgage and tenement'. Its location, within the Market Place, suggests that this was one of the original burgages created under the charter. Although the property seems to have incurred the standard burgage rent, the width of the Staircase House plot was roughly one and a half times that of many others on the Market Place.[28]

The cruck-framed building occupied an area between the north side of the Market Place and sloping ground to the rear. Indeed it seems that, when the Market Place was laid out in the thirteenth century, sufficient level ground for building upon was deliberately left at the front of the burgage plots on this side. It is unknown whether any structures existed to the rear of the cruck-framed building. On the outer side of the stone and tile wall footings are the remains of a cobbled surface of the same period (2.15).

Further to the rear, a garden-type soil has been discovered beneath a sixteenth-century addition to the property. Together this evidence suggests that there was a cobbled yard immediately behind the building, above the slope, and that the rear of the burgage plot was given over to a horticultural use.[29] Excavations to the rear of No 33, the eastern neighbour of Staircase House, also uncovered a garden-type soil, in this case overlying a broad gully containing late medieval pottery.[30]

Archaeological investigations within the footprint of the cruck-framed building at Staircase House have revealed a small number of shallow gullies and possible post-holes which contained

Above: 2.15 Staircase House, the remains of an outer wall of the 1460 house, and stone cobbling of a medieval yard

28

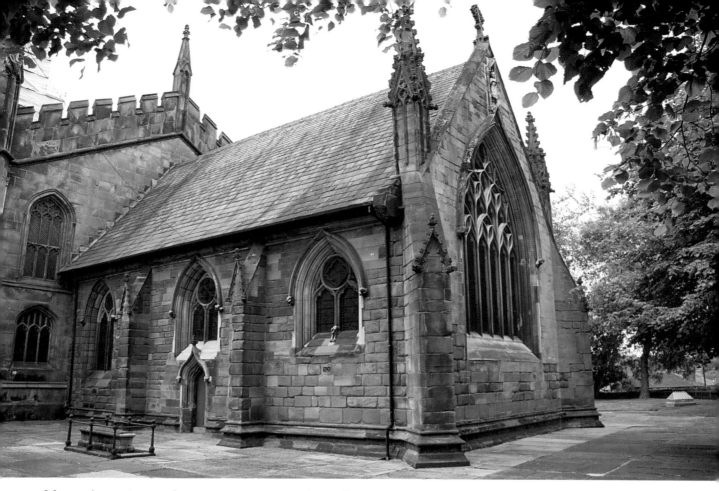

fifteenth to sixteenth-century pottery. These features may be no earlier than that building but the same area also produced thirteenth to fourteenth-century pottery, belonging to an earlier phase of activity on the site. Tree-ring dating has shown that some of the timbers of a later roof above the cruck-framed building were actually felled in the late thirteenth or early fourteenth century, in other words they were reused from an earlier structure. This evidence is not conclusive but it does suggest that an earlier building had stood on this site, erected perhaps not long after the creation of the medieval borough.[31]

Above: 2.16 St Mary's Church, the medieval chancel

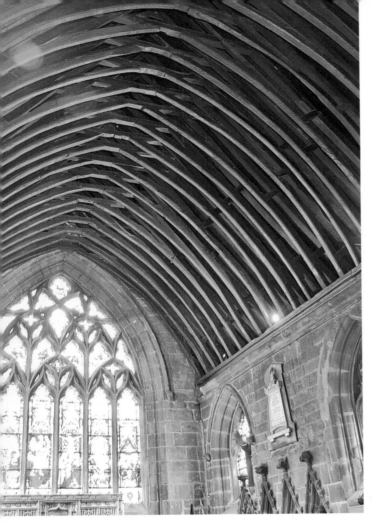

At present, the occupants of the cruck-framed building are unknown. While there is a surviving list of the names of the owners and occupants of burgages in 1483, it is not possible to single out Staircase House within either this or later lists of the sixteenth century. However, from the relative size of the burgage plot it seems likely that the property was occupied by a person of some wealth and esteem. A possible candidate is William Dodge, a member of a local family of merchants whose prosperity was based on the region's early textile trade. In 1483 he owned six burgages in the town, including his own residence on the Market Place.[32]

St Mary's Church

By the end of the medieval period by far the largest building in the town was the parish church of St Mary, which dominated the east end of the Market Place. It is probable that the church was founded in the twelfth century, when the creation of the barony gave Stockport a new importance.
A Matthew 'cleric of Stockport' who was living in the late twelfth century may have been its earliest known rector, a distinction which otherwise goes to Richard 'parson of Stockport' in about 1230. The twelfth-century church would have been built in the Norman style of architecture but no evidence of it has survived. The parish was a large one, perhaps because of the relatively sparse local population at the time of the church's foundation. However, as the population later expanded in the new borough and the surrounding countryside, the income of the rector from tithes increased considerably and made Stockport one of the wealthiest churches in Lancashire and Cheshire.[33]

Above: 2.17 The roof of the medieval chancel

The present church of St Mary, for all its Gothic appearance, is largely the result of a rebuilding programme in 1813-17. The chancel survives from the medieval church but has been restored (2.16). It is built in the Decorated style of English architecture which flourished in the last quarter of the thirteenth century and the first half of the fourteenth. Responsibility for the building and upkeep of a church chancel lay with the rector, and the quality of Stockport's chancel

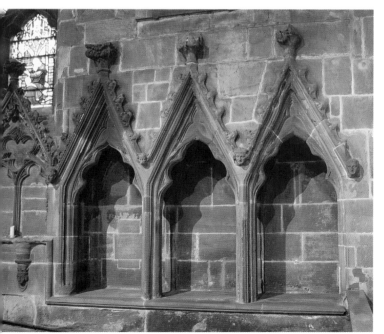

reflects the growing revenues from the parish. The chancel retains its medieval timber-arched roof (2.17) and its triple sedilia (stone seats for the clergy) and double piscina (a stone basin used for washing the communion vessels) (2.19). In the nineteenth century the architect Augustus Welby Pugin described the sedilia as being among the most beautiful examples in England. The north wall contains a niche, originally either an Easter sepulchre or a tomb canopy, which now contains the carved effigy of Richard de Vernon (2.18).

Above: 2.18 The effigy of Richard de Vernon, rector between 1306 and 1334, who is believed to have built the chancel
Left: 2.19 The medieval sedilia (the seat for the clergy) and double piscina (stone basins)

31

This was originally placed within a chapel built outside the south wall of the chancel, which was taken down in 1812. De Vernon, a younger son of the baron of Shipbrook, was rector of Stockport between 1306 and 1334 and is traditionally identified as the builder of the chancel. There are also remnants of a chapel on the north side of the chancel incorporated within a nineteenth-century vestry. The remainder of the church, demolished in the early nineteenth century, is shown on early paintings (2.20). A plan of the nave and tower in 1810 has also survived (2.21). The nave had a western window in the Decorated style, as were the windows in the low side aisles. The windows of the clerestory, that is the part of the nave walls which rose above the aisles, were of a later date. These were in the Perpendicular style, which spanned the

Above: 2.20 The old St Mary's Church by William Shuttleworth, circa 1810

period from the second half of the fourteenth century to the early sixteenth. They were possibly inserted in about 1536 when Nicholas Elcock of the town bequeathed money towards 'the building of two aisles now in hand'. The tower, which stood at the north-west corner of the nave, dated from the early seventeenth century.[34] After its demolition, the bells were acquired by the newly built church of All Saints in Marple where they still hang in the church tower. A pew from the old St Mary's Church belonging to the Davenport family is now in the chapel at Bramall Hall, their former home (2.22).

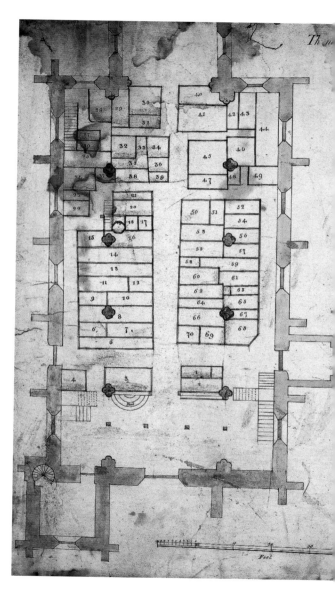

Above: 2.21 The nave and tower of the old church, a plan of 1810
Below: 2.22 The Davenport pew in Bramall Hall chapel, originally the family pew in St Mary's Church, Stockport

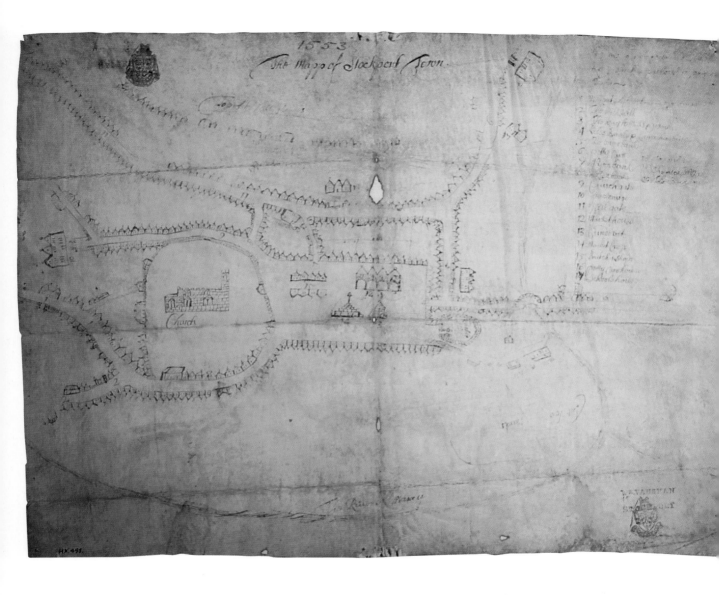

Above: 3.1 'The Mappe of Stockport Town', drawn in about 1680

3. 'A populous and great markett towne', 1500-1700

In the sixteenth and seventeenth centuries the economy of the town was becoming more diverse.[1] By 1500 Stockport was firmly established as a centre of the region's early textile industry, and it continued in this role in the following centuries. By 1610 the town had even given its name to a type of linen called 'Stopport cloth'. In the seventeenth century two of the town's other key industries had begun to take root. One of these was hatting, the other was a rudimentary silk industry. These early industries were carried out in domestic workshops and laid the foundations of the later factory town. The buildings of the town were also being transformed. From the second half of the sixteenth century Stockport was influenced by a national revolution in house design which has been called the Great Rebuilding. In and around the Market Place there are still a small number of timber-framed buildings which were a product of this transformation, including Staircase House.

It is from this period that we also have the earliest known map of the town. It is believed to date from about 1680 and was probably commissioned by the lord of the manor.[2] The map depicts the buildings in a pictorial form and, although many are shown in a stylized manner, some effort has been made to depict the town's more distinctive features (3.1). In 1661 Stockport could be described as 'a populous and great markett towne'.[3] There were about 305 households in the town in 1619, suggesting a population of 1400-1500.[4] The population was roughly the same in 1664, when Stockport seems to have been the fifth largest town in Cheshire behind Congleton, Macclesfield, Nantwich and Chester (by far the largest with a population of about 7500).

In the mid seventeenth century Stockport was a centre of Parliamentarian support during the English Civil War. On the 25th of May 1644 the war came to the town, when a Royalist army under Prince Rupert advanced on Stockport from the west. Outside the town, the smaller defending force was able to offer only limited resistance before withdrawing across Lancashire Bridge. One local man rose to particular prominence during the Civil War period. John Bradshaw, originally from Marple within Stockport parish, served as the president of the court which tried King Charles I in 1649, and later, from 1649 to 1651, was President of the Council of State, the highest office in the country (3.2).

'A great market and much frequented by dwellers far remote'

In about 1620 William Webb, in his description of Cheshire, wrote of Stockport that 'it is a great market and much frequented by dwellers far remote'. In a similar vein it was recorded in 1634 that the market attracted a 'great concourse of people' to the town.[5] Traders at this period included people from Manchester, itself a thriving market town.[6] The weekly market dealt principally in grain, other basic foodstuffs and goods, and livestock. As one commentator summed it up in the 1670s, the town 'hath a considerable market for corn and provisions on Friday'.[7] At some date prior to 1633 the market had been moved from Thursday, the day specified in the market charter of 1260.[8] Among local farmers selling or buying surplus crops in the seventeenth century was John Ryles of High Greaves, near Gatley, who recorded in his diary variations in the market price of oats, barley, wheat and beans.[9] Details of the market are also known from the records of Stockport's manorial court, the court leet, which survive from the 1660s. Its unpaid officers included two 'market lookers', who were tasked with bringing traders who infringed the market regulations before the court. Charges included using inaccurate weights and measures, selling grain outside the set time which was signalled by the ringing of a bell, and allowing pigs to stray before being sold (3.3). Two 'officers for flesh' were tasked with protecting

Left: 3.2 John Bradshaw, originally of Marple, the presiding judge at the trial of King Charles I

36

against the sale of unwholesome meat.[10] To help regulate the market, different types of traders were allocated different areas in the Market Place. In the 1660s the space around the market cross, for example, was reserved for producers from outside Stockport to sell commodities such as 'butter, cheese, eggs, pullen [poultry] and the like', although it is known that some locals tried to claim this for themselves by setting up their own stalls.[11]

By the early seventeenth century Stockport also had a number of retail shops. While the market principally dealt in foodstuffs and livestock, the shops stocked non-perishable goods and luxury items. A man might, for example, buy a new sword or dagger from James Tellier (Taylor), the cutler, or in the 1640s visit the shop of the bookseller, stationer and bookbinder Edward Harpur. Some shopkeepers often had a combination of stock, so that apothecaries, and dealers in textiles and hats might also sell groceries such as soap, starch, spices and honey.[12] Among the most lucrative shops were those of the drapers, men who specialised in the sale of fabrics. The will of the draper Nicholas Elcock, compiled in 1620, shows that he was owed money by over 160 individuals.[13] Many, if not all, of these debts may represent goods sold on credit. The people owing the money came not just from the town but also a broad surrounding area which included north-west Derbyshire as well as north-east Cheshire, including places near Maccles-field. Those from Lancashire were mostly from the area to the south of Manchester, a larger town than Stockport and as a market and retail centre probably Stockport's main rival.

Above: 3.3 Entries for the 'market lookers', in the manorial court record for May 1663

The journal of Henry Bradshaw of Marple, the brother of Judge Bradshaw, for the years 1637-44 records his expenditure on his many trips to Stockport, which frequently fell on the Friday market day. Goods which he bought at Stockport in the year 1641 included rat poison, 'a purse leather', garden seed, shoes and gloves for his daughter Katherine and son Henry and leather to mend his own shoes, wheat, ear wires, wooden platters, 'Scottish cloth', gloves, 'pins points and laces', tobacco including some' for Poynton colliers', a bridle and stirrups, a cart saddle, apples, wheat, meat, hemp, calf skin, pepper, and paper. The range of items listed in the journal shows that Henry Bradshaw used market days to buy goods from Stockport shops as well as from the market. The market day could also be a social occasion and a number of entries in the journal refer to money spent on dining and in the tavern. Henry also made many, but less frequent, visits to Manchester and much more occasional visits to Macclesfield.[14]

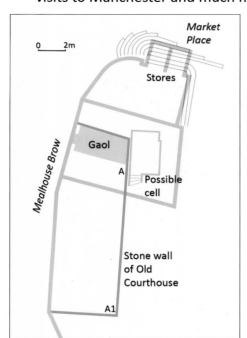

Stockport must have been busiest during the time of the fair, or rather fairs. In 1633 King Charles I gave permission for two more such gatherings, in addition to the ancient fair held in October. They were to be held on the 20th and 21st of April and the 10th and 11th of July, and the grant included the right to hold a 'court of piepowder', a court specifically called to settle disputes arising out of the fair. The July fair was later discontinued. The April fair, following the change of the calendar in 1752, moved to the 1st of May, and by the early nineteenth century had developed into a great festive occasion.[15] By the late seventeenth century the Park, the area in the bend of the river to the north-west of the Market Place, was used for the fairs, and perhaps in particular for the sale of livestock.[16] Cattle markets were still being held in this area in the mid nineteenth century, when the pastureland of the Park had given way to the streets of the industrial town.

The Old Courthouse: Stockport's earliest town hall

By the sixteenth and seventeenth centuries we have evidence for buildings which were specifically used to help conduct the market, and to administer the town. The earliest known of these was situated on the south side of the Market Place, at the top of Mealhouse Brow. This was the location of the town's early lock-up or dungeon which continued in use until 1790,

Above: 3.4 Plan of the Old Courthouse at Mealhouse Brow

and on Mealhouse Brow evidence of this still survives in the form of a small cell, opening directly onto the street. Recent renovation and rebuilding works have uncovered new informa-tion about this site. The cell was found to have been constructed within the ground floor of a two-storey building, roughly 14.5m long and 4.5-5.0m wide, which had once extended away from the Market Place along the east side of Mealhouse Brow. This had been built with stone walls of well-made courses of the local sandstone, which were preserved within a later brick building on the site. The east wall was only one course thick but had survived to the full two storeys, about 5m in height (3.4-3.6). The walls are believed to date from the fifteenth or sixteenth century.[17]

Stone buildings at this period were rare within the town and this structure must have been of some importance. Differences in the stonework show that, in its present form, the cell was not an original feature. Its north and east walls seem to be formed by the walls of the early stone building. The south wall is later and possibly dates from the eighteenth century, when the brick-vaulted ceiling was probably also built (5.6, 5.7). However, there was a gaol at Stockport in 1607, and in 1692 a lease was made of

Above: 3.5 The stone east wall of the Old Courthouse
Below: 3.6 The east wall of the Old Courthouse as first uncovered and recorded in 1998

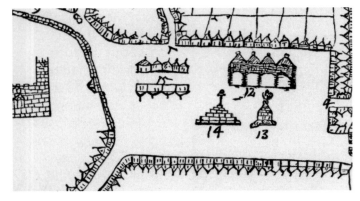

'the Old Courthouse and the 2 litle rooms adjoyning with a room under called the Dungeon being an ancient inn adjoining to Winbank'.[18] At this period Wynn Bank was the name of Mealhouse Brow and it is very probable that the stone building was the Old Courthouse of the lease, making this Stockport's oldest municipal building. It would have been of a general type found in other towns, comprising a two-storey building of which the upper floor was used for meetings of the court leet, held twice a year. This floor would also have served as the centre of administration of the market, the place where the official weights and measures were kept. The lower floor included the town's lock-up, as was the case at the early town halls at Liverpool (built in about 1515) and Warrington (perhaps built in the late fifteenth century).[19] At Stockport a mealhouse, that is a place from which meal was sold, is documented in 1545 and may have been part of the Mealhouse Brow building or an even earlier structure.[20]

The Market House

In the seventeenth century a new administrative and market building was built, located more conveniently within the Market Place itself. It was known as the Market House and stood towards the west end of the Market Place. It is shown on the Stockport map of circa 1680 as comprising a colonnaded ground floor and an enclosed upper floor, which was surmounted by gables (3.7). This is a familiar type of market hall and town hall, and similar colonnaded buildings are known, for example, at Liverpool (built 1673-5) and Wigan.[21] It was recorded in 1752 that the upper room of the Stockport building, 'the Market House Chamber', housed the official weights and measures used to regulate the market (3.8).[22] In the seventeenth century this room probably also became the venue for meetings of the court leet in place of the 'Old Courthouse' on Mealhouse Brow.[23] In 1752 bread and salt were sold from the Market House, which also contained the stalls of two local hatters. This may also have been the designated place for the sale of bread a century earlier, since in 1663 several traders were fined for sitting at or near 'the courthouse in the Market Place, selling bread and other merchandise'.[24]

Above: 3.7 The Market Place on the circa 1680 town map. Key: 4 - Kelso Banke (Bridge Street Brow); 7 - Wynn Banke (Mealhouse Brow); 8 - Rosen Banke (Rostron Brow); 12 - Market House; 13 - Cundeuet (Conduit); 14 - Market Cross; 15 - Butchers Shops

The Shambles and the Meal and Cheese House

Meat was sold from the 'shambles' or butchers' shops at the east end of the Market Place. They are mentioned in manorial records of the late 1620s to mid 1640s[25] and are shown on the circa 1680 map as two parallel rows of buildings running from the direction of the church. The northern row seems to have been demolished by 1770 (4.1). The southern row of shambles was still standing in the early nineteenth century, when William Shuttleworth's painting of the Market Place shows them to have been fairly substantial structures of two storeys (3.9). One of the shambles in 1732 was described as comprising a shop with a chamber above it and a cellar beneath.[26] In Shuttleworth's day one was still a timber-framed building but others seem to have been rebuilt in brick.

Subsequent to the drawing of the circa 1680 map a new building was built at the east end of the Market Place. In the later part of its working life, and perhaps from the outset, this was the Meal and Cheese House and was used by local farmers for the sale of those two commodities. The building is shown on William Shuttleworth's painting as brick-built, of two storeys, with twin gables facing into the Market Place (3.9). The upper floor contained a single large room, accessed by an entrance on the north side of the building. In the early nineteenth century the ground floor was occupied by four shops, divided by a central passage-way.[27] Its gabled appearance suggests that the building was constructed in the late seventeenth or early eighteenth century.

Above: 3.8 Official weights and measures for the manor and barony of Stockport. These examples date from 1824-6.
Below: 3.9 The Meal and Cheese House (left) and shambles (right) on William Shuttleworth's painting of the Market Place, circa 1810

The Market Cross, Conduit and 'Plague Stone'

On the north side of the Market Place in the seventeenth century stood two other structures. The more easterly of these was the market cross, which is shown on the circa 1680 map as a simple cross, no doubt of stone, raised on six steps. The cross is documented in 1654, when marriage banns were announced here on successive market days. Its form suggests that it may have been medieval in origin.[28] In the late seventeenth and eighteenth centuries a number of the old market crosses in local towns such as Manchester and Salford were replaced by more elaborate structures. It is possible that a replacement was also proposed for the old Stockport cross but the scheme was not actually implemented.[29] Proclamations were still being made from the cross in the eighteenth century but it seems to have been removed by 1770.[30]

To the west of the cross was the 'conduit', which provided a public supply of water. This is shown on the circa 1680 map as a free-standing stone-built structure (3.7). It would appear to have been gravity-fed from a spring rather than the water being pumped from a well. In 1690 the overflow water was leased out to supply the area to the north-west of the Market Place known as the Park, then still largely grazing land. In the 1700s the 'waste water' was leased to John Shallcross of Staircase House, possibly for the same use.[31] Later in the eighteenth century water from the conduit was being used for a different purpose. It was noted in 1778 that 'in the market-place stands a conduit, from whence, by means of leaden pipes, the houses are supplied with water, in the same manner as at London'. John Aikin similarly reported in 1795 that spring water was carried 'by pipes to different parts of the town, as well as into the houses on the rocks in the market-place'. The source for this supply system lay in the Barn Fields on the opposite side of the Tin Brook valley, and to reach the Market Place must have involved a very circuitous route.[32] In the 1820s the town was provided with a new water supply, derived from an artesian well at the Park Mills.[33]

Right: 3.10 A wooden water pipe from Stockport

Recent archaeological investigations have shown that houses on the north side of the Market Place also had their own private wells.[34] Early wooden water pipes have also been found in the town (3.10).

A rectangular stone, hollowed into a shallow basin, is said to have been found in the Market Place and is believed to have been used to contain vinegar in which coins were 'disinfected' to prevent the spread of plague (3.11). During an outbreak of the plague in 1605-6 the Stockport parish register recorded the burials of fifty-one people whose deaths were attributed to the disease; the vast majority, if not all, of the deceased lived within the town itself.[35]

Public Punishments

The Market Place was also a place for public punishments. The stocks were located here and it was also here that, when required, the pillory and the whipping post, or 'rogues post', were set up. The right to enforce such punishments initially belonged to the lord of the manor and was confirmed in 1500, when the pillory was described as the penalty for fraudulent bakers.[36] By the seventeenth century the cases heard by the lord's court, the court leet, were punished by fines and included public nuisances and assault, as well as infringements of the market laws and regulations. Cases for which corporal punishment could be imposed were now heard by the county magistrates or, until about the late seventeenth century, by Stockport's mayor.[37] The burgess Thomas Wrasse in 1661 was placed in the stocks for challenging the authority of the mayor William Beeley, but responded by bringing a charge of assault.[38] Responsibility for maintaining the various forms of punishment lay with the lord of the manor. In 1664 the court leet found it necessary to order the lord to repair the 'cage' (possibly a reference to the dungeon on Mealhouse Brow), the stocks, the whipping post and the ducking stool.[39]

Public punishments were still being administered in the town in the early nineteenth century. The whipping post was used as a penalty for petty theft, in addition to a prison sentence, and the punishment was carried out on a Friday market day. In July 1822 the public whipping of James Brown, found guilty of stealing a linen apron, was halted and moved from the Market Place

Above: 3.11 The 'plague stone'

because the spectators were a hindrance to normal business. The pillory, which was a punishment for perjury, forgery and similar offences, may have been last used in Stockport in 1801 when Ellinor Elkin was sentenced to be placed there for one hour for receiving stolen goods. The stocks were at one time located near the church gates, but were moved to the top of Mealhouse Brow and later to the west end of the Market Place. In August 1822 two women were placed in the stocks in the Market Place for three hours, one for 'scandal', the other for being drunk, failing to pay the fine and being abusive to the magistrates.[40] The town's stocks have not survived, although local examples exist at Bramhall, Marple and Mellor (3.12).

Scolding or swearing women could be silenced by the 'brank', or scold's bridle. This was an iron contraption which fitted over the head and had a spiked bar which held down the tongue, and a leather strap attached which was used to lead the offender (3.13). 'Bridling' was listed in 1692 among the punishments which traditionally had been imposed by the mayor, along with the whipping post and ducking stool. At a later

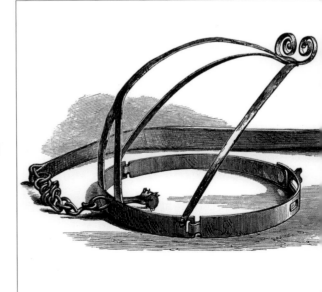

Above: 3.12 In the stocks at Bramhall
Below: 3.13 The Stockport brank, or scold's bridle

date, the brank seems to have been particularly associated with keeping order in the Market Place and, when not in use, it was hung as a warning at the door of the collector of the tolls.[41]

Staircase House and the Great Rebuilding

Stockport is fortunate in having no fewer than three timber-framed buildings which survive relatively intact from the Great Rebuilding of the sixteenth and seventeenth centuries. One is Underbank Hall, once the property of the Arderne family of Harden Hall in Bredbury, whose fine facade is set back from Great Underbank (3.15). In the early seventeenth century, a group of service buildings were located at its rear, on a site now occupied by a banking hall.[42] Another is the Three Shires, also on Great Underbank, once a house belonging to the Leghs of Adlington Hall (3.14). It includes a street range and a large timber-framed rear wing, now masked by later brick walls. The third is Staircase House on the Market Place, and there are also surviving fragments of timber framing in a fourth property, No 20 Market Place which was formerly the Angel Inn.

The Great Rebuilding is perfectly exemplified by Staircase House, which was remodelled and extended on several occasions in the sixteenth and seventeenth centuries (3.16, 3.17).[43] In the first of these, the medieval cruck-framed house was converted into a post and truss building, that is with a frame of upright and horizontal timbers

Above: 3.14 The Three Shires, Great Underbank
Below: 3.15 Underbank Hall, the former town house of the Ardernes

45

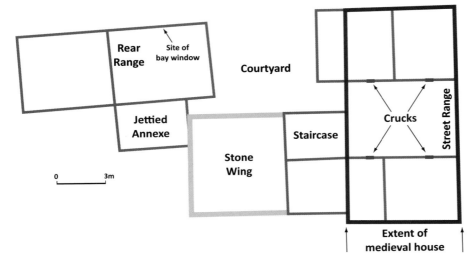

Rear Range

Site of bay window

Courtyard

Jettied Annexe

Stone Wing

Staircase

Crucks

Street Range

0   3m

Extent of medieval house

Left: 3.16
Staircase House as rebuilt and enlarged in the sixteenth and seventeenth centuries
Below: 3.17
A reconstruction of Staircase House in about 1700, looking south towards the Market Place

carrying the roof structure. This allowed the building to be raised to a full two storeys, with a facade distinguished by decorative timberwork and triple gables as at Underbank Hall. To its rear a new timber-framed wing contained a staircase, the predecessor of the elaborate feature which later gave the building its name. This was at a time when access to the upper floor in many lesser houses in the town would have been by a ladder. Perhaps at the same time, a detached outbuilding was added further to the rear. It originally seems to have been of only a single storey.

Later the main house was further extended to the rear by the addition of a stone wing (3.18). The choice of material may have been a precaution against fire. The kitchen of the house was located in this wing and had a wide stone fireplace (3.19), with a side niche for the dry storage of salt. At about the same time that the stone wing was built, the detached outbuilding was raised in height to three storeys. There is evidence that the new upper storey had a bay window, looking out to the east. In the past it has been suggested that this building served as either workshops or warehousing but it may simply have provided additional accommodation.

From the evidence of tree-ring dating, these various changes probably began in the mid to late sixteenth century and possibly continued into the early years of the seventeenth. Currently the occupants of Staircase House at this period are unknown. One possibility is that it was a residence of the Elcock family.[44] The Elcocks rose to prominence as Stockport textile merchants and are known to have owned burgages on the Market Place. In the mid sixteenth century a fortuitous marriage transformed the head of the family into the manorial lord of Whitepool near Nantwich, but family members maintained a presence in Stockport into the seventeenth century.

Above: 3.18 The staircase wing (left) and stone wing (right) at Staircase House

These later residents included Dorothy Elcock, the widow of the lord of Whitepool, who may possibly have lived at Staircase House until her death in 1613.

In 1618 other alterations were made to Staircase House which further embellished what was already a high status residence. They can be dated with some confidence, thanks to tree-ring dating and an ancient datestone in the building inscribed with the year 1618 and the initials 'S' and 'MJE' (3.20). The major alteration was the replacement of the sixteenth-century staircase

Above: 3.19 The kitchen fireplace in the stone wing at Staircase House

with the richly carved Jacobean staircase which gave the building its present name (3.21). This was also an opportunity to add another storey to both the timber-framed wing which contained the staircase, and the adjoining stone wing. Its new storey was built in a pink sandstone distinct from the yellow sandstone of the original building (3.18). The room above the kitchen was now decorated with timber panelling.

As a result of recent research, the occupants of Staircase House from this time until the early eighteenth century are known.[45] In 1619 the building was occupied as a dower house by Mary Shallcross, the widow of Richard Shallcross of Shallcross Hall, near Whaley Bridge in Derbyshire. It was for her that the improvements of 1618 were undertaken, and the initials on the datestone are those of Mary, her elder son John and Edmund her younger. Edmund Shallcross was later appointed as rector of Stockport parish, but in the Civil War he was charged with being a Royalist supporter by local Parliamentarians and his property was confiscated. In July 1644,

Above: 3.20 The 1618 datestone at Staircase House with the initials of Mary Shallcross and her sons, John and Edmund

while travelling to London to plead his case, Edmund was killed during a skirmish near Dudley Castle. His mother lived until 1652 and after her death Staircase House was used as a town house by three successive generations of the Shallcross family. Her son John (d. 1673) probably made the final timber-framed addition, a jettied annexe to the rear building. From 1676 until its sale in 1732 it was the property of his grandson, also named John. He seems to have spent much of his time at his Stockport residence, where he entertained other members of the gentry. The diary of William Davenport of Bramall Hall in the 1700s records several visits to 'Cuz Shallcross'. In addition to Staircase House, he owned or leased a considerable amount of other land in and around the town, including a swathe of largely agricultural land behind the north side of the Market Place, extending from Millgate to the Mersey. He made his own improvements to Staircase House, fitting decorative panelling in the upper rooms of the street range (3.22). Until the 1920s the adjoining house at No 33 Market Place contained identical panelling, along with a staircase with twisted balusters of a similar date (3.23, 3.24).[46]

Above: 3.21 The Jacobean staircase at Staircase House

Left: 3.22 The panelling at Staircase House added by John Shallcross the younger in the late seventeenth or early eighteenth century
Below left: 3.23 The panelling at No 33 Market Place
Below right: 3.24 The staircase at No 33 Market Place

Buildings and People of the Market Place

In 1619 some 39 households were listed as living on the Market Place, accounting for about an eighth of the town's population (3.25).[47] The figure is very close to the number of properties which existed in the Market Place before alterations in the mid nineteenth century, probably reflecting the longevity of many of the property divisions. The 1619 list, which was drawn up to record Easter offerings to the parish church, may follow a clockwise route around the Market Place, beginning in or close to the south-west corner.[48] The head of one of the households is described as a butcher, and seven others as traders. Of this last group five may have lived on the north side of the Market Place as neighbours of Mary Shallcross, with Robert Hardman and then Thomas Leigh to her west, and John Barret, and then Nicholas Elcock, and Roger Harpur to her east. We also know something about the residences of two of these men from the inventories of their goods compiled after their deaths. The house of the draper Nicholas Elcock seems to have principally consisted of a shop and a living room or parlour, with upper-floor rooms above. The house of the mercer Roger Harpur was situated on the corner of the Market Place and Millgate. In the 1640s it included three main ground-floor rooms and a kitchen, five upper-floor rooms including a 'New Chamber' and the 'Millgate Chamber', together with a dairy house and a warehouse.[49] One of the other known traders on the Market Place in 1619 was Raph Roson who very likely lived at No 1 the Market Place adjacent to Rostron Brow or, as it is named on the circa 1680 map, 'Rosen Banke'. The other known trader, William Taylor, probably lived a few doors down towards Wynn Bank, the present Mealhouse Brow. A timber-framed building stood at No 1 Market Place until the late nineteenth century, when it was taken down and rebuilt as an aviary in Vernon Park (3.26, 3.27).[50]

Thomas Elcocke
Robert Cottrell
Olyver Dodge
Thomas Butler
John Robinson
James Hunt
Alice Cartwright
John Spooner
Henry Dickallson
Widow Hunt
Widowe Johnson
John Johnson
Widowe Robinson
Thomas Leigh trade
Robert Hardman trade
Marie Shalcross widow
John Barret trade
Nicholas Elcocke trade
Roger Harp trade
Raph Roson trade
Edward Brodhurst
Grace Bennetson
Widowe Smith
William Taylor trade
Widowe Siddall
Edward Wood
John Tompson
John Wynne
John Hough
Robert Hough butcher
Francis Mosse
Thomas Mosse
William Warburton
Anne Burdsell
Samuel Siddle
George Jennings
John Martindale
William Hartley
Frances Lee

Left: 3.25 The heads of the households on the Market Place in 1619

In the seventeenth century at least two public houses are known to have stood on the Market Place and there are likely to have been more. The Bull's Head was standing in about the 1690s when it was occupied by Mary Wild. Next door was the White Horse, which was acquired by a draper who rebuilt the property.[51] Stockport's inns, as well as providing food and drink for visitors to the town and market, offered stabling for their horses, and numerous entries in the journal of Henry Bradshaw are for payments made to ostlers, stablehands working in local inns.

Above: 3.26 The former timber-framed No 1 Market Place
Below: 3.27 The aviary in Vernon Park, about 1900

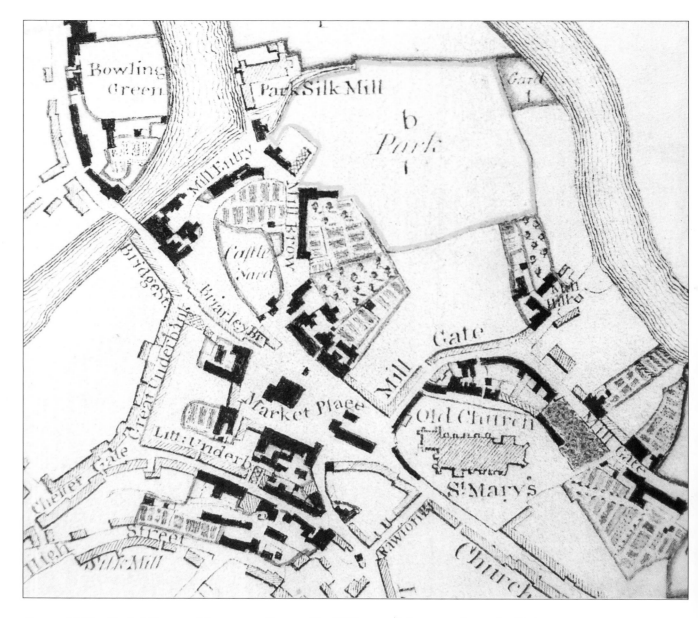

Above: 4.1 The Market Place and its surroundings on the 1770 map of the town, drawn for Sir George Warren
Facing page: 4.2 Stockport in about 1790, a town of houses, churches and factories

4. The Market Place of the Silk Town, 1700-1780

In the eighteenth century the silk industry made Stockport one of the region's first centres of the Industrial Revolution.[1] At the beginning of the century there was already a small-scale silk industry in and around the town, which included the production of yarn and the manufacture of silk buttons. In 1732 the shape of this industry was transformed, when the North-West's first water-powered textile factory was built in the Park below the Market Place (4.1). The mill produced silk yarn using machines of a design which had been smuggled out of Italy by John Lombe of Derby in about 1716. His half-brother, Thomas Lombe, obtained patent rights over this machinery in 1718 and monopolized its use until the patent's expiry fourteen years later, when a partnership of six wealthy individuals financed the building of the Park Mill in Stockport. Macclesfield followed with its first silk mill in 1743-4 and Congleton in 1753. At Stockport the industry expanded and by the early 1770s there were four large water-powered silk mills in the town, employing over a thousand people, while another six hundred worked in other smaller silk works. This was at a time when the total population of the town was in the order of four to five thousand. The impact of the eighteenth-century silk industry on Stockport was profound.
It created for the first time a large body of factory workers in the town and changed the town's very appearance (4.2). One account of 1769 spoke of 'the large silk mills, belonging to the chief tradesmen of the place...`Tis here the raw silk is chiefly thrown and prepared for the Spitalfields weavers'. This was also a town 'inhabited by a great number of gentry, and well filled with ware-house-men, who carry on the check, mohair button, and hat manufactories'.[2]

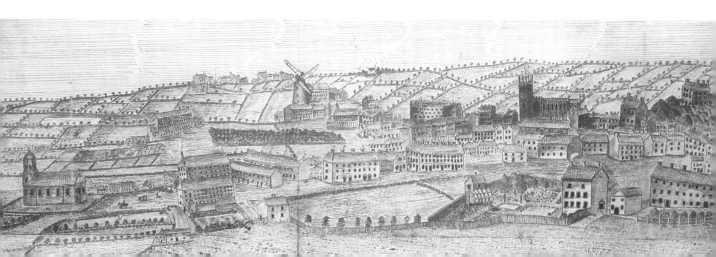

By the early eighteenth century cotton was also part of the town's textile industry, and was initially carried out in domestic workshops, producing checks (fabrics with a cotton weft and a linen warp). In the 1770s the local cotton industry began to be transformed by new machinery, and in the second half of the decade Stockport's first water-powered cotton factory, Castle Mill, commenced operation. In the 1780s cotton would replace silk as Stockport's main industry, leading to the growth of the town on an unprecedented scale.

The Market and Fair at Work

By the 1760s corn grown in the fields around the town was no longer sufficient to meet the needs of its inhabitants, and more needed to be brought in

Butchers	6d	'Potts'	1d
Butchers (that are burgesses)	5d	Shoemakers (4)	2d (own standings)
Gingerbread Sellers	2d	Breeches	3d
Hosiers	3d	Tanners (10)	8d 'a dicker'
Tobacconists	3d	Sheep pens	1s 0d a piece
Hardwares	4d	Ballad Singers, Petty Hawkers and 'Soceris'	Pay 2d, some 3d each
'Gardiners'	2d		

In the Market House

Bread	2d	(Worsley) Hatter	5d
Salt	1d	(Jepson's) Hatter	1d

At the Toll Bars

Sheep pay 8d a score
Cattle pay 3s a score or 2d a piece
Horses & Colts pay 2d a piece

All persons who find their own Standings usually pay 1d each for Toll in the Market days...pay double at a Fair.

'Standings during Fare'

Gingerbread	Single stand	4d
	Double stand	6d
Hardware	Common size	1s 6d
	Pewter 1s 2d	
	(Stevenson own)	2d

from further afield.[3] John Aikin in 1795 listed Stockport, Manchester and Macclesfield as the chief markets for the surplus grain grown in Cheshire. Of Stockport's market he wrote, 'A great quantity of corn and oat-meal are sold at it, and it is accounted the best market for cheese in the country'. Oatmeal, made into bread, cakes and porridge, was an important part of the diet of the less well-off, that is the majority of the local population.[4] Cheshire was already famous for its cheese in the seventeenth century, the main product of an agricultural economy based

Above: 4.3 Rents for market 'standings' or stalls, 1752

predominantly on cattle rearing and dairy farming. As well as being sold to local consumers, it was also exported to more distant markets. Much of the cheese produced in the county was sent to London, particularly through the ports of Chester and Liverpool. Stockport's cheese market is known to have attracted buyers from Yorkshire. In 1769 the town was described as having 'a large market on Friday, remarkable for the vast quantity of cheese from hence bought up for exportation'.[5] As we shall see, surviving accounts for the 1780s imply that several hundred tons of cheese were sold in the market each year. In the case of other provisions, there was increasing pressure on the market to meet the needs of a growing local population. Aikin noted that there had been a time when surplus oatmeal was brought to Manchester from Stockport, and when the price of meal and corn in Stockport's market determined that in Manchester's. In the mid eighteenth century traders at Manchester's Saturday market included a sizeable group of Stockport butchers, who may have been selling meat left over from Stockport's market the day before. Their attendance at Manchester seems to have decreased from the 1770s, perhaps as a result of a rising demand in their home town.[6]

We know something of the range of produce, goods and livestock on sale in the Market Place in the mid eighteenth century from a document of 1752 listing the rents for 'standings', that is stalls or space rented by market traders.[7] These included charges for butchers, clothes dealers and shoemakers, hardware and pottery dealers, 'gardeners', gingerbread sellers, tobacconists, 'petty hawkers', ballad singers and 'sorcerers' (4.3). Bread and salt were sold at the Market House, the colonnaded building on the west side of the Market Place, where two hatters, Worsley and Jepson, also had stalls. In 1739 there were 63 stalls owned by the lord of the manor, and another thirteen owned by the people who used them.[8] Gingerbread sellers and hardware dealers were singled out for higher charges at the fair when they also had the option of hiring a longer stall, suggesting that both were particularly lucrative businesses at fair time. Sheep, cattle, horses and pigs were also sold at the market and fairs.

In 1752 a charge of 1 shilling was made for the hire of a sheep pen, while during the fair sheep were allowed to stand unpenned at a charge of 4d for twenty animals. Pig sellers were charged 1d for 'Ground in the Fare'. Tolls for livestock were collected at toll bars set at various points of entry in and around the town, at Lancashire Bridge on the north, Millgate and Churchgate on the east, Petty Carr (the area of Chestergate) and School Bridge (on the Tin Brook at the entrance to Great Underbank) on the west, and Hillgate on the south. In the early 1730s tolls from livestock accounted for the majority of the manorial revenue collected from the fairs.[9]

By the mid eighteenth century the number of fairs was on the increase. As a result of the change in the calendar in 1752, the original medieval fair moved to the 23rd October. By 1769 there were three other fairs. One was held on the 1st of May and was the surviving one of two additional fairs granted by King Charles I. Two others were held on the 4th and 25th of March. Precisely when they were established is not certain, but John Warren was already seeking to add two fairs towards the close of the seventeenth century and the aspiration was shared by his son Edward at the beginning of the eighteenth.[10]

Sir George Warren and the Market

In the 1760s and 1770s the collection of market tolls was one of many causes of complaint against the lord of the manor, Sir George Warren. He held the lordship for much of the eighteenth century, and on his death in 1801 was buried in Stockport parish church where his memorial can be seen on the wall of the chancel (4.5). It was for Sir George that the first reasonably accurate plan of the town was surveyed in 1770 with the particular purpose of showing the properties under his ownership (4.1). He had inherited the lordship of Stockport from his father who died in 1737, when George was aged two. At this date the Warren family was in severe financial difficulty, and George was saved from this situation only by the astute actions of his guardians. This reversal of fortune was completed in 1758 by his marriage to the wealthy heiress Jane Revell. She died in 1762 and it is his second wife, Frances, who appears with him and his daughter Elizabeth in the family portrait by George Romney (4.4). Despite his new financial security, Sir George was determined to draw as much profit as possible from his position as lord of the manor of Stockport. As the town was growing so were the revenues which might be claimed for the manorial coffers. Unfortunately for Sir George, attitudes in the town were also changing and he faced an opposition led by manufacturers and tradesmen who were relative newcomers and had no longstanding sense of loyalty to the manorial lord.[11]

In the case of the market, cheese mongers were seen by Sir George as a particularly lucrative target. It was a long-established requirement that cheese brought for sale in the market should be weighed on the lord's scales and charged a toll of 1d a hundredweight (1 cwt). Under Edward Warren, Sir George's father, the right to collect the cheese toll had been leased out to William Hambleton. He was the landlord of the Ship Inn on the Market Place, and from him the lease of both the toll and the inn passed to Peter Bostock. Both men applied this levy to burgesses and

Facing page: 4.4 The Warren family, by George Romney, circa 1769

non-burgesses alike. By the 1760s the collection of the cheese toll was back in manorial hands and the lack of exemption for burgesses was added to the list of grievances against Sir George's administration.[12] The burgesses had originally been the small group of individuals who owned a burgage plot within the medieval borough but now all property owners in the town were required to be enrolled as burgesses in the court leet and to pay Sir George 5 shillings for the privilege.

In addition he was faced with the problem that a number of cheese and meal mongers from outside the town were now conducting their business from hired rooms and shops in and around the Market Place and were refusing to pay toll and stallage. Sir George's response was to threaten to move the market to one of his fields on the edge of the town.[13] Perhaps it was to avoid such difficulties that in 1776 he leased the collection of all revenue from the market and fair to a Thomas Boardman. He paid £100 for this right and is said to have made a loss, but the tolls seem to have been leased out again in 1785. Accounts from 1780-4, when the collection was back in the hands of the manorial authorities, show that after expenses the market and fair generated an income of about £70 a year.[14] These accounts include annual receipts from cheese of between £25 8s 5d and £29 11s 5d, which at the toll of 1d per hundredweight represent about 300 to 350 tons being weighed each year on the lord's scales. We do not know how much escaped the toll

Above: 4.5 The memorial to Sir George Warren in St Mary's Church

collector. Reliable figures for total cheese production in Cheshire are difficult to come by but estimates in the early nineteenth century ranged from 9700 to 11,500 tons per annum.[15]

Alterations to the Market House

In 2008, during the restoration of the nineteenth-century Covered Market, archaeologists found the remains of an earlier rectangular structure. It was 5.5m (6yds) long and 3.6m (4yds) wide and had sandstone walls about 0.3m (1ft) wide, which in part were set on a foundation of handmade bricks (4.6). The interior contained the remains of a clay floor. Fortunately the date of the structure could be established by pottery and glass of the early to mid eighteenth century which was found within its brick foundation.[16] Its location lies on the west side of the Market Place, within the footprint of the seventeenth-century colonnaded Market House as shown on the town plan of 1770. On the evidence of the finds, the excavated structure was added in the mid eighteenth century, and the most likely interpretation of the walls is that they are the footings of a chamber which would have risen to the ceiling of the ground floor of the Market House. This would have created an enclosed area with a sunken floor within the otherwise open-sided space. Given Sir George Warren's stance on the Market Place, it is possible that he made this addition to the old Market House to help enforce his levy on cheese mongers, with cheese being kept here prior to being weighed or sold.

Above: 4.6 Excavating the eighteenth-century Market House structure

Above: 4.7 Castle Mill, a late eighteenth-century view
Facing page. Above: 4.8 Castle Mill and St Mary's Church, about 1790
Below: 4.9 Castle Mill, 1831

Castle Mill and Sir George Warren's Shambles

Sir George Warren's main contribution to the development of the Market Place area was the construction in the 1770s of Castle Mill, the first water-powered cotton mill built in Stockport and one of the earliest in the region. The country's very first such mill had been erected in 1771 by Richard Arkwright at Cromford in Derbyshire, and housed the spinning machines of his own invention, known as water-frames. From 1776 Arkwright was constructing new mills and making a very considerable fortune. His success may well have prompted the

construction of Castle Mill in Stockport, which was completed by September 1778.[17] It was built on Castle Yard, which had been the site of the medieval castle and was still the property of the lord of the manor. In the early 1770s this was a vacant space, surrounded by a stone wall, while next to its entrance was a smithy which had been built by Sir George's father adjacent to the market.[18] The mill was constructed at Sir George's own expense, with the intention that the building would then be leased out. The design of Castle Mill was possibly unique. Arkwright's mills were rectangular in plan. It was a form which was probably adopted from the silk industry and which remained the norm for textile mills into the twentieth century. Castle Mill was circular, or more precisely oval, with a central

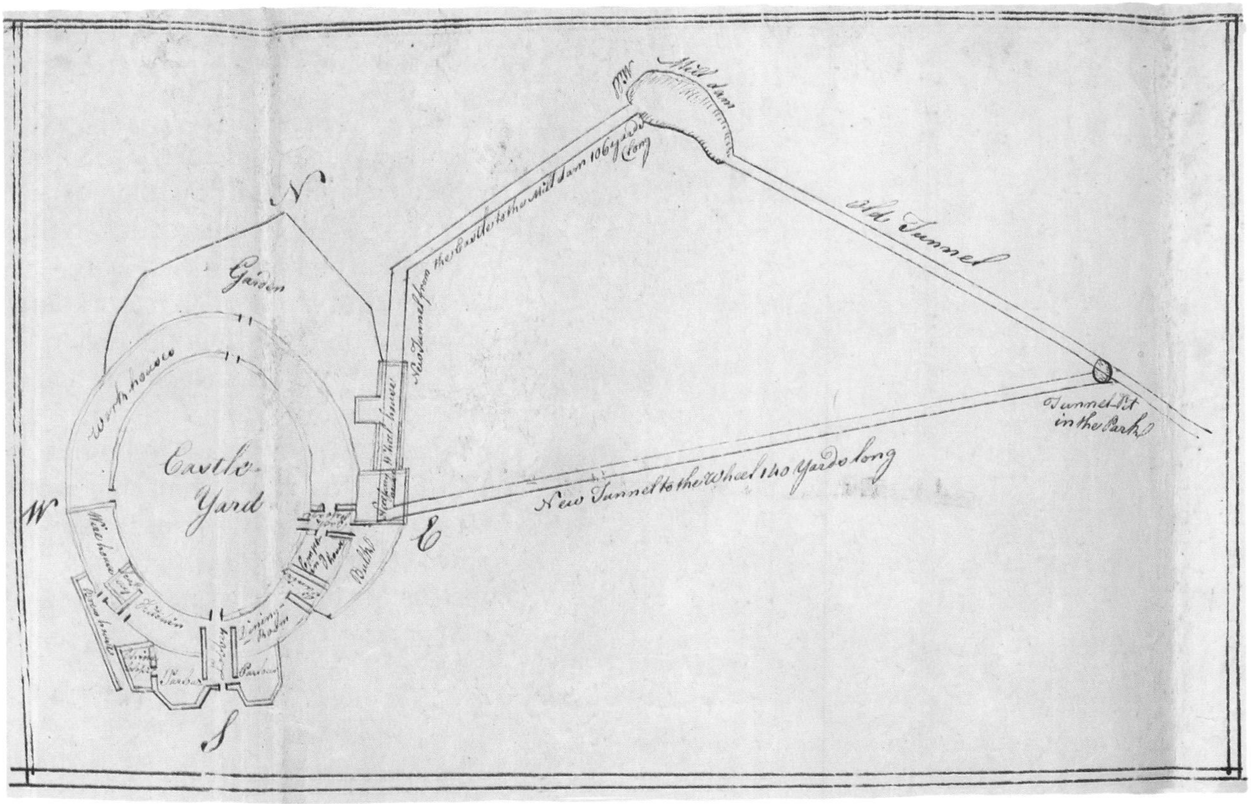
N
W
E
S
Mill dam
Old Tunnel
New Tunnel from the Castle to the Mill dam 106 yards long
Garden
Castle Yard
Tunnel Pit in the Park
New Tunnel to the Wheel 140 Yards long

courtyard, and its walls were crowned with battlements. The mill was brick-built, at least three storeys in height and must have dominated the west end of the Market Place, as the church dominated the east (4.7-4.10).[19]

The mill was not Sir George's first idea for the site. In February 1775 he entered into an agreement with John Broadhurst, a Stockport bricklayer, and George Astley, a local joiner. They were to enclose an oval area of Castle Yard with a brick wall, 18ft (5.4m) high, with battlements, and against the inside of this they were to build fifty butchers' stalls or shambles, also of brick with a slate roof. Each was to measure 9ft by 6ft 8in (2.7m by 2m), and was to have a door enabling the stall to be locked; facing this, on the outside wall, was to be a shuttered window, square on the

Above: 4.10 Castle Mill and its tunnels, 1778
Facing page: 4.11 The tunnels to the Park Mills, on a map of 1850

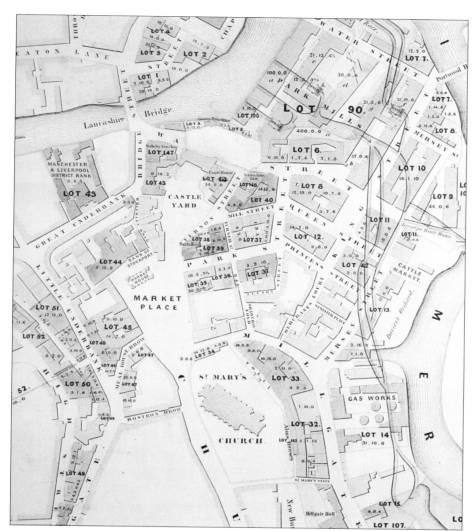

inside but round on the outside and at least 3ft (0.9m) in diameter. A covered colonnade of octagonal wooden pillars was to run around the front of the stalls, facing onto a central courtyard. Each stall was to be numbered and fitted with a wooden counter, chopping block and hooks for hanging the meat.[20] It is unknown how far this project had advanced before the decision was made to build the cotton mill or to what extent its fabric was incorporated within the new building.

The design of both the shambles and the mill was no doubt influenced by the fact that the medieval castle had once stood on this site but it may also have been an expression of Sir George's own temperament. In 1767 he had planned to construct a new industrial building, probably a silk mill, close to the River Mersey on the west side of the town. There was strong local opposition to the fact that this would have been built on common land, and the scheme was abandoned.[21] Given Sir George's stormy relations with a number of the townspeople, the battlemented appearance of both the shambles and Castle Mill could have been intended as a reminder of his authority. Those battlements and the round windows, planned for the shambles and perhaps included within the mill, may also have been designed for a practical purpose. In 1779 a depression in the textile trade saw workers attacking several mills in Lancashire. At Stockport, in anticipation of an attack which in the event failed to materialize, 'the Castle Cotton works once more become a place of arms, and the embrasures filled with Sir George Warren's cannon, which commanded Manchester Hill, Stockport Bridge, and the ford of the Mersey'.[22] The Reverend John Watson, who owed his rectorship of Stockport's parish church to Sir George, praised the mill as 'a large beautiful round building'. John Byng who visited Stockport in 1790 took a different view, describing it as 'looking like one of the grandest prisons in the world'.[23] The mill was not entirely given over to cotton production. The eastern side of the battlemented building contained part of a 'dwelling house', and included a kitchen and dining room. The front part of the house was contained within an adjunct to the mill. Here, to either side of a central entrance hall, was a parlour heated by a marble fireplace and with a great bay facing onto the Market Place.[24]

The mill was driven by a wooden waterwheel, described in 1778 as being 40ft (12.1m) in diameter and 6ft (1.8m) in width. This was situated in an external wheelhouse, on the Vernon Street side of Castle Hill (4.10). In about 1742, a new millrace had been constructed to take water from the River Goyt to the mills in the Park, below Castle Mill, and its course ran in a tunnel to the north of the Market Place. A branch tunnel was driven from this to the Castle Mill wheelpit from where a second new tunnel carried the water back to the Park Mills. When new cotton mills were later built in the Park, other tunnels were added to this system (4.11).

Above: 4.12 Inspecting the Castle Mill wheelpit

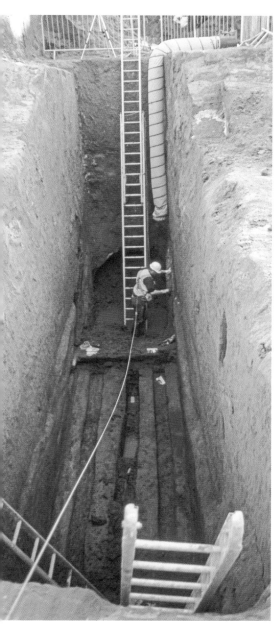

The first occupant of Castle Mill in 1778 was John Milne, who is believed to have installed pirated versions of Arkwright's machinery in the building. Within a few months of the mill's opening, Milne's family was in secret negotiations to set up Arkwright-type machinery in France, and in 1782 Milne himself moved to the Continent. After his departure, Castle Mill continued in use as a cotton mill but in 1791 Sir George Warren and Henry Marsland of the Park Mills agreed that water-power should cease to be supplied to Castle Mill in nine years time.[25] The building's design may have contributed to this early demise. Power in mills was transmitted from the waterwheel to the machines via a series of gears and vertical drive shafts and horizontal line shafts. It was a system to which the rectangular blocks of other mills were admirably suited, but which in an oval building may have introduced all manner of practical difficulties.

Following its closure as a mill in 1800, the building was used for the sale of the fashionable fine cotton cloths known as muslins and was open for business every Monday and Friday.[26] The production of these materials was made possible by Samuel Crompton's invention of the 'mule', the first machine capable of producing a fine enough yarn, which he first made public in 1780. Muslin manufacture was introduced to the Stockport area in about 1784, very probably by Samuel Oldknow, and for a number of years was a key part of the local textile industry. It has sometimes been supposed that Castle Mill was built as a muslin mill, but its construction predates the muslin industry by several years. The muslin hall was itself short-lived and by 1810 had ceased to operate.[27]

Above: 4.13 Recording the wheelpit

Another use to which the building was put had a longer life. The 'dwelling house' on the side of the mill facing the Market Place had been built with a brewhouse attached and in 1800, if not before, it became an inn. In April 1800 the Castle Inn was the scene of a meeting of local textile manufacturers. This was later immortalized by William Radcliffe, who publicly volunteered on that occasion to invent new machinery to increase the productivity of handloom weavers.[28] The resulting devices led Radcliffe into bankruptcy but were adopted for powerloom weaving and in the early nineteenth century helped establish Stockport as the first great centre of that industry.

Rediscovering the Castle Mill Wheelpit

In 2003 a refurbishment of Castle Yard and a new development on the site of Castle Mill provided the opportunity for an archaeological investigation. At Castle Yard this revealed evidence for the levelling and lowering of the site in the mid nineteenth century following the demolition of Castle Mill but found no in-situ remains of the mill itself. The area of the former Courts between Vernon Street and Warren Street proved more productive. This was known to have been the site of the mill's waterwheel and here the back-filled remains of the mill's wheelpit were first identified during a watching brief, and were then fully excavated (4.12, 4.13).[29]

Above: 4.14 The headrace and the inclined sluice
Below: 4.15 Looking towards the tailrace

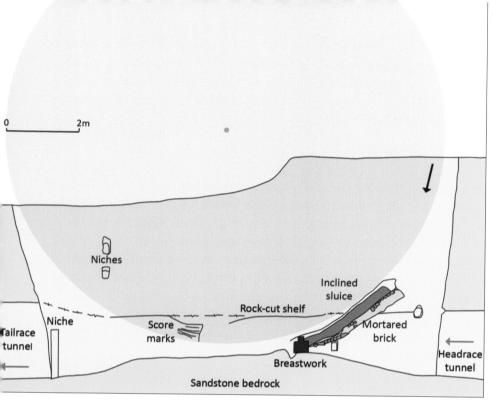

The wheelpit was a deep rectangular pit, with slightly tapering sides, which had been cut into the natural sandstone on the flank of Castle Hill and provided sufficient room for the 40ft (12.1m) diameter waterwheel and a sluice mechanism. When originally discovered the wheelpit had a maximum recorded depth of over 7m. Before the wheelpit could be safely excavated it was necessary for the uppermost part to be removed but this still left a pit which was about 6m deep (4.16).

The position of the wheel within the pit was evident from score marks on one of the side walls. The sides and base of the pit also contained a number of slots and niches deliberately cut into the bedrock as part of the wheel's construction or operation. Because of the waterlogged conditions, a number of timbers had also survived either as part of these rock-cut features or within the material at the base of the pit. Water had entered the wheelpit through an arched headrace tunnel at the south end and exited through a tailrace tunnel at the other (4.15).

In front of the headrace tunnel, set in the wheelpit sides were the remains of an inclined sluice which funnelled the water over a low timber breastwork and onto the wheel (4.14). The arrangement is typical of a wheel with buckets, and part of the outer wooden rim (or 'sole board') onto which they would have been fitted was found within the base of the wheelpit. This is one of the earliest (if indeed not the earliest) examples of this type of waterwheel to have

Above: 4.16 The east elevation of the wheelpit showing the approximate position of the 40ft (12.1m) diameter waterwheel

been discovered, and the technology shows an advancement on waterwheels of the true under-shot type which were turned by the force of water striking the wheel's wooden paddles. At its base the width of the wheelpit was reduced to about 1.85m by a rock-cut shelf on either side, just sufficient to accommodate the 6ft (1.8m) wide wheel and presumably designed to minimize the amount of water escaping around the wheel's sides.

The Buildings of the Market Place

In 1790 John Byng remarked of Stockport that 'All the old houses of this town were formerly built of oaken timber; this, now, in general has given way to brick', adding that his own lodging place, the old White Lion on Great Underbank, was 'striped and barr'd with as much black timber, as would build a man of war'.[30] Brick had been used only sparingly in the seventeenth century but from about the 1710s it was adopted as the material for new buildings in the town.[31] In time most of the town's old timber-framed buildings were also rebuilt in brick. The greatest period of this rebuilding seems to have been the late eighteenth century and the early nineteenth, but some earlier instances are known. The rectory, which overlooks both the Market Place and the church from higher ground to the east, was rebuilt as an imposing three-storey brick house by

the rector Samuel Stead in about 1743, the date recorded on a rainwater head. The same year could be found on a rainwater head at No 7 Market Place, formerly the Sun Inn, whose facade was largely rebuilt in the late nineteenth century (4.17). (During renovation and rebuilding works in the early twenty-first century, the early rainwater head was replaced by a modern head with the same date). At Staircase House there is no clear evidence of any new building in the early or mid eighteenth century. No 33 Market Place, immediately to its east, on the other hand, may have been one of the earliest brick buildings in the town, to judge from its late seventeenth to early eighteenth-century decorative panelling and staircase, and from the apparent use of internal timber framing (3.23, 3.24).

Above: 4.17 The 1743 rainwater head at No 7 Market Place

There is also a tradition linking this building with the Jacobite rebellion of Bonnie Prince Charlie. In late 1745 Jacobite troops crossed the River Mersey at Stockport and Cheadle during their march south towards London. About a week later, after that advance was abandoned at Derby, they returned to Stockport on the retreat north. It is said that on this occasion a rearguard was billeted for one night in the town under the command of Lord Elcho and that he chose the Market Place building for his own accommodation.[32]

In 1731 there were at least four inns on the Market Place, the Sun, the Ship, the Black Swan and the Bull's Head.[33] As well as being a place of commerce and residence, the Market Place was also a place of industry. In 1768 among the silk mills in Stockport was Tetlock's, on the Market Place.[34] It was one of a number of smaller mills in parts of the town with no obvious water-supply to drive the machinery. If this mill was not simply hand-operated, it may have been literally horse-powered, with the animal harnessed to, and turning, a mechanism known as a 'gin' (a shortened form of 'engine'). Some of these smaller mills may have been set up in existing buildings. Evidence for a different form of industrial site was discovered at Shawcross Fold in the late nineteenth century, when workmen uncovered a number of early bricks and tiles. They included a type of perforated tile which would have formed the floor of a kiln used for drying oats or malt. This area was developed with housing and other buildings from about the mid 1780s, and it seems likely that the remains belonged to an earlier eighteenth-century drying kiln (4.18).[35]

Above: 4.18 A perforated tile from Shawcross Fold, used in a corn-drying or malt kiln

Above: 5.1 'A forest of chimneys shoot into the air', Stockport in about 1835

5. The Market Place of the Cotton Town 1780-1840

Between the 1780s and 1830s Stockport underwent a truly massive expansion which was largely due to its key role within the region's cotton industry.[1] In the 1780s, within a few years of Castle Mill beginning operation, three of the town's large silk mills were given over to cotton. The early 1790s saw a burst of new mills, so that in 1795 the town was said to contain 23 large cotton factories, as well as a large number of workshops used for spinning. Stockport's ample supply of water-power was crucial to the early growth of its cotton industry but steam-powered mills were also being built from the early 1790s and coal was made more readily available by the opening, later in the decade, of the Stockport branch of the Ashton Canal. In the late eighteenth and early nineteenth centuries only Manchester may have surpassed Stockport as a cotton-spinning centre. From 1803 Stockport industrialists pioneered the development of the powerloom, so that the town also became the first great centre of powerloom weaving. In the early nineteenth century it also had a growing reputation for its hatting industry and had the beginnings of an engineering industry, as well as the residual remains of its once great silk industry. However, these other forms of manufacture were very much secondary in importance to the cotton industry, which was now by far the single largest employer of the local population.

The population of Stockport in 1780 was about 5000. By 1800 the number had at least trebled to become the largest of any town in Cheshire. The area of the town also underwent an unprecedented expansion, new streets were laid out behind the old thoroughfares, nowhere more so than on Hillgate, and new industrial suburbs developed outside the old Stockport boundary, at Portwood, Edgeley and Heaton Norris. In the 1820s growing congestion within the town even led to its first bypass, Wellington Road, now the A6. It was built by the Manchester and Buxton turnpike trust on the western fringe of the town but quickly became a focus for new development. In appearance Stockport was now the very epitome of a mill town. 'Mills and factories rise out of the dense mass of houses', said one account in 1842, 'and around, a forest of chimneys shoot into the air' (5.1).[2] Stockport was made a Parliamentary borough in 1832 and a municipal borough in 1835 with boundaries which included its new suburbs, and had a total population in 1841 of 50,000 (5.2).

The Worker as Consumer

At the heart of this industrial town lay the ancient Market Place, depicted by the local artist William Shuttleworth in a painting of about 1810 (5.3).[3] By that time the presence of a large working-class population was already having a significant influence on the character and organization of trade in the town. At some point between 1795 and 1810 the decision was made to hold the market not only on Friday, its traditional day, but also on Saturday. The Friday market was used by farmers for the sale of cheese, oatmeal and other produce to dealers. The market on the following day was a more local affair. Here the townspeople bought meat and other provisions, with trading continuing until eleven thirty at night. The arrangement was of obvious benefit for factory workers, whose working week did not finish until Saturday afternoon, when they were also paid.[4] In the early nineteenth century foodstuffs were also being bought by the working class from numerous small local shops. These were easy to set up with little more than the front room of a house being required. Their success owed much to the fact that they sold food on credit but they also had a reputation for overcharging.[5]

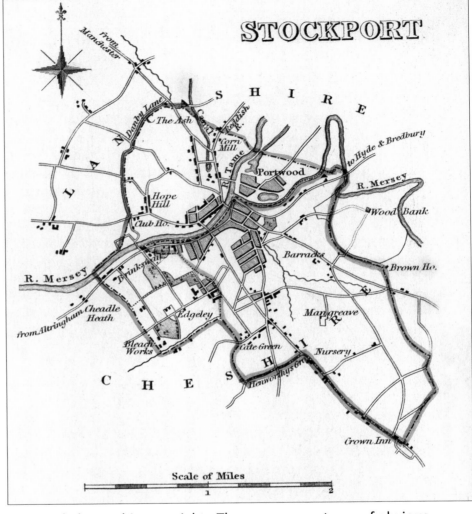

Above: 5.2 The Parliamentary and municipal borough, 1835

Collecting the Tolls

Small provision shops seem to have first appeared in about the mid eighteenth century, a time which also saw private rooms being used as alternative places for dealers in cheese and meal to conduct their trade. In some Cheshire towns, by the beginning of the nineteenth century, corn had effectively ceased to be sold on the open market as transactions between farmers and dealers changed to private contracts struck often in inns.[6] These changing patterns of trade all threatened to deprive the lord of the manor of revenue from the market. In the 1770s and 1780s Sir George Warren had chosen to rent out the right to collect the tolls. For at least part of the early nineteenth century his successors followed suit, so that from 1811 to 1840 this right

Above: 5.3 The Market Place, by local artist William Shuttleworth, circa 1810

was leased first to Thomas Moore and then to his son of the same name.[7] In 1822 and 1838 the steward of the manor published a list of the tolls which the collectors were entitled to charge (5.4). The amounts remained unchanged between the two years, and were copied from an earlier list of about 1802.[8] The printed lists show a doubling of the toll for weighing cheese since 1770 and an increase in stallage since 1752. They also show the manorial response to the rise of the new places of trade, stipulating that 'All persons bringing meal, flour, cheese, potatoes, or other produce, and unloading the same at any shop or other place in the town, on market days, are liable to pay toll for the same'.

Under the Moores, the printed lists of tolls were rarely shown to the traders from whom payment was exacted. One commentator in 1843 was of the opinion that 'The amount of tolls has always depended more on the cupidity and gullibility of the collector and payer than upon any fixed principle'. In the same year, William Stride, who began his

Above: 5.4 The market tolls, 1838

A

LIST OF TOLLS,

TO BE TAKEN AND PAID

To the Right Honourable George John Warren, Lord Vernon,

On Fair Days and Market Days,

AND STALLAGE, &c. ON OTHER DAYS,

AT STOCKPORT,

IN THE COUNTY OF CHESTER.

GRAIN of all sorts, to have one Dishful taken from each Load.
FLOUR to have one Dishful taken from each Load.
MEAL of all sorts, to have one Dishful taken from each Load.

	s.	d.
For the Ground whereon are Stalls of 6 feet long, or less - - -	0	6
For ditto ditto from 6 to 12 feet long - - -	1	0
For ditto ditto above 12 feet long - - -	1	6
On other Days in the Week, each Stall - - - - - -	0	3
Weekly Stalls, of 6 feet, for Apples, Greens, and other Vegetables -	1	6

Double Stalls, double Money.

	s.	d.
Hogsheads, each - - - - - - - - - - - - - -	0	3
Tierces, each - - - - - - - - - - - - - -	0	2
Panniers and Baskets, with Butter, Geese, Fowls, &c. each - - -	0	1
Fish Stalls, each Day - - - - - - - - - - -	0	6
On all other days - - - - - - - - - - - -	0	3
Carts, with Fish, Peas, Nuts, Fruit, or any other kind of Vegetables, each -	0	4
Auctions on Carts, and all other Auction Stands, each to pay -	1	0
On other Days - - - - - - - - - - - -	0	6
Potatoes, Turnips, Carrots, &c. per Load - - - - -	0	1
Pigs, per Drove - - - - - - - - - - -	0	1
For each Pig sold, the Purchaser to pay - - - - - -	0	4
Earthenware Lots, of 8 feet long, or less - - - - -	0	4
For all Lots above 8, and not exceeding 12, each - - -	0	8
For Cows, Bullocks, and Heifers, brought for Sale, the Bringers or Buyers to pay for each - - - - - - -	0	2
Calves, Sheep, and Pigs, to pay each - - - - -	0	1
Each Hundred Weight of Cheese, for Weighing and Warehouse Room, to pay -	0	2

The above Tolls to be paid on demand, to the Clerk of the Market, or his Deputy.

All Burgesses regularly admitted at the Courts held within the Manor, are exempt from Toll *on the regular Market Days only*, in respect of Stalls of the usual size, namely, 6 feet in length; and in respect of Flour, Grain, &c. exposed for Sale on those Days in the Market House; but such Flour, Grain, &c. must be removed at the end of every Market Day out of the Market House, unless the Clerk of the Market shall permit it to remain there for a longer period.

All Persons bringing Meal, Flour, Cheese, Potatoes, or other Produce, and unloading the same at any Shop or other Place in the Town, on Market Days, are liable to pay Toll for the same, as above.

THOMAS ASHWORTH,

Agent and Receiver for the Manor and Barony of STOCKPORT aforesaid.

STOCKPORT, December, 1838.

LOVE AND BARTON, PRINTING OFFICE, 10, MARKET-STREET, MANCHESTER.

toll-collecting career as an agent of the Moores, recalled that the sums charged in the weekly market were generally in line with the printed list but he also admitted to some irregularities. On some streets, tolls were charged on produce delivered to shops on non-market days. Hawkers were charged a toll on market day wherever they were found within the town and irrespective of whether they were selling foodstuffs or other goods from their baskets or barrows. The fair also gave the collectors a certain freedom, with charges being agreed with the holders of individual stalls or shows based on the size of plot, its location and the duration of their stay. Similar agreements were made with the owners of the butchers' stalls in the Market Place. Toy sellers and bazaar owners, on the other hand, were charged an extra fifty per cent for a stall at the fair. In all cases, those who refused to pay tolls or stallage could have goods or other paraphernalia confiscated until the money was forthcoming.[9]

A 'spacious and convenient' Market Place?

John Aikin in 1795 described the Market Place as 'spacious and convenient'. Some local people would not have agreed. In 1785 a scheme was put forward to improve the state of the town and the Market Place was one of the priorities. Trade had increased so much that the site was overcrowded. The situation was not helped by the Market Place's naturally uneven surface and the narrowness and steepness of the surrounding streets. A decade earlier, Sir George Warren's proposal for fifty new butchers' shambles on Castle Yard might have offered some improvement, but a change of plan had resulted in the construction of Castle Mill in their place. The scheme of 1785 was dropped before it gained Parliamentary approval, possibly because of opposition from local ratepayers but perhaps because of Sir George. The proposed improvements would have been financed initially by the sale of Stockport's common land, and this ran against the interests of Sir George who had been disposing of plots for his own profit. He had entered Parliament in 1761 as MP for Lancaster, and it may not be coincidental that the improvement scheme was launched during the one short break in his Parliamentary career.[10]

One alteration which was made in the late eighteenth or early nineteenth century was the removal of the colonnaded Market House at the west end of the Market Place. The precise date and circumstances are unknown, but the building was still standing in 1770 and is not shown on William Shuttleworth's painting of the Market Place in about 1810. Its administrative functions now seem to have passed to the more cramped building standing at the east end of the Market Place which was also used as a Meal and Cheese House. Later in the nineteenth century, the Stopfordian John Greenhalgh recalled that 'It was here where the archives of the town were kept, and where the civic authorities met to transact the town's business'.[11]

The End of the Mealhouse Brow Gaol

Among the improvements which had been proposed in the scheme of 1785 was the building of a new gaol to replace that on Mealhouse Brow. The proposal was no doubt influenced by the rising number of offenders as the town's population expanded, but contemporary ideas on the need to improve prison conditions may also have played a part. In 1787 the county magistrates agreed to contribute funds for a new gaol, and Sir George Warren provided the site, a plot of land on the bank of the River Mersey close to Lancashire Bridge. Work on the new building began in 1790. Like the old gaol, this was only a place of temporary confinement. Inmates included vagrants, sent here as a punishment, and people who had been arrested for more serious crimes and who were waiting to be brought before a magistrate. Lengthy sentences of

Above: 5.5 The entrance to the gaol on Mealhouse Brow

imprisonment were served at the gaols in Knutsford or Chester.[12] One of the last inmates of the old gaol on Mealhouse Brow is believed to have been John Dean, a Stockport hatter who was arrested in 1790 for the murder of his wife in Watson Square, off Hillgate. Dean was tried at Chester, found guilty and executed there. His body was brought back to Stockport, where it was gibbeted on a gallows on the Great Moor.[13]

In 1790 the Mealhouse Brow gaol was described as 'a very unhealthy and incommodious place for the confinement of any prisoners'.[14] The cell which still exists on Mealhouse Brow comprises a barrel-vaulted chamber about 4m long, 2m wide and just under 2m high, entered from the street by a low door (5.5-5.7). In the late nineteenth century this retained its old oak door, fitted with an iron grating to let in light and air.[15] Immediately to its rear is a possible second cell in the form of a small basement room, accessed via steps from the floor above (3.4).

Above and below: 5.6 & 5.7 The gaol interior, 'a very unhealthy and incommodious place'

The Improvements of 1818-20

The most level approach to the Market Place is from the east along Churchgate, but originally this narrowed alongside the churchyard of St Mary's. Under an Act of Parliament in 1801 Churchgate also became part of a turnpike route between Stockport and Marple, which continued across the north side of the Market Place where its line was marked out by stone setts (5.8).[16] In 1818 the bishop of Chester gave permission for 385 square yards (322m²) to be removed from the churchyard and added to Churchgate. The nave and tower of the church had just been rebuilt and the intention was to improve the setting of the building by giving this side of the churchyard a more regular appearance. This required the removal of a number of burials, most of which were reinterred in a new graveyard to the east of the church (5.9).[17] The scheme also involved the removal of a row of lock-up shops belonging to the lord of the manor which stood alongside the churchyard wall and added to the congestion.[18] Once Churchgate was widened, new stalls were set up here for a potato market.[19]

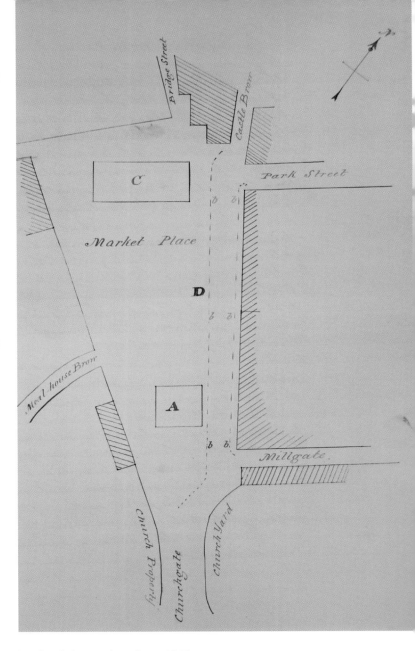

Above: 5.8 The course of the turnpike on the north side of the Market Place, 1842

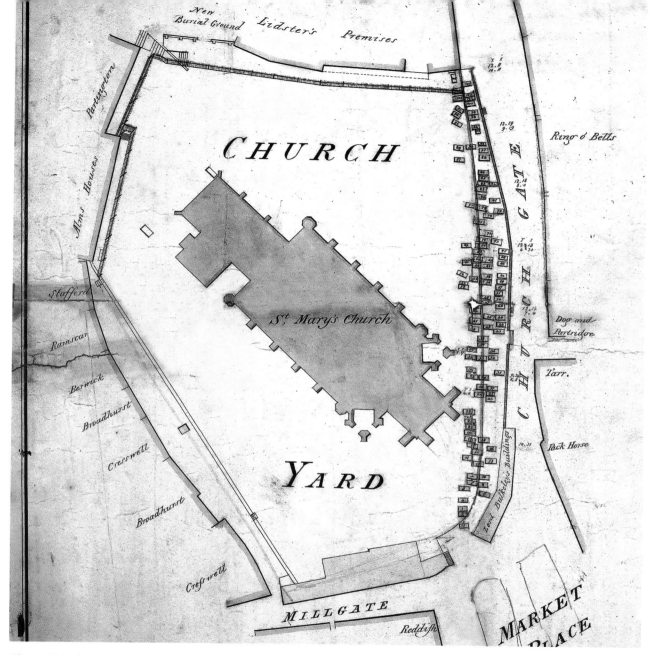

Above: 5.9 The widening of Churchgate, 1818

Responsibility for the repair of the Market Place lay with Stockport's surveyor of the highways. In about 1820 he had the whole surface repaved and a broad footpath made around its southern and western sides.[20] A level footway, raised on steps, still runs along these two sides. Remains of an early cobbled surface were found below the Covered Market in 2008 and may also have been

Above: 5.10 The entrance to Mealhouse Brow, about 1960

part of the 1820 improvement (5.11).[21] The unevenness of the Market Place was at its most extreme on the south where ground levels dip at the entrance to Mealhouse Brow. This allowed single-storey extensions to be built out from the neighbouring properties, either as part of the 1820 improvement or as a separate scheme (5.10). The larger of these extensions was situated on the east side of the Mealhouse Brow entrance and was roofed by its own area of pavement, accessed by its own steps. The space below those steps was also put to use, for they are carried on small arched chambers which have sometimes been identified as additional cells within the Mealhouse Brow gaol but seem to have been used simply as storage (3.4, 5.12).

The New Meal and Cheese House, 1823-4

The first half of the 1820s was a boom period in Stockport's cotton industry, which saw many new mill buildings spring up and the town's powerloom-weaving capacity increase threefold. The prosperity of this time may have been a significant factor behind the alterations to the Market Place which were now carried out. Another influence may have been the establishment in 1822 of the town's first newspaper, the *Stockport Advertiser*, which provided a new platform for local sentiments. It was also a period when technology was bringing its own changes, with gaslights now being installed in private houses in the town, beginning with the Market Place area in 1821.[22]

Above: 5.11 An old cobbled surface of the Market Place, uncovered below the Covered Market
Below: 5.12 The 'cells' below the steps outside No 8 Market Place

The outstanding complaint about the Market Place was the condition of the buildings which stood at its east end and comprised the Meal and Cheese House and the shambles. The *Stockport Advertiser* reported in 1824 'It has long been a desirable object to remove these buildings, which dirty and filthy in appearance, were a great nuisance to the Market Place, and made the entrance to the Churchgate and Millgate both narrow and inconvenient'. Such was the state of the cheese market that buyers who had previously travelled from Yorkshire no longer attended and for several years Stockport had been losing business to Manchester.[23] By 1823 the mealhouse had been transferred from the Market Place building to a room above the old gaol on Mealhouse Brow. Meetings of the manorial court were also now held there, although it was, in the words of the *Stockport Advertiser,* 'a poor unplastered room, hardly superior to the meanest stable in the town, and all the assembly in danger of knocking their dignified heads against the ceiling, or metamorphosing their blue surtouts into the flourly habiliments of a dusty miller'.[24] The court, so it seems, had returned to the ancient meeting place of the Old Courthouse, although it is likely that by this date its stone walls had been subsumed within the present larger brick building. To provide a more fitting venue, in 1823 the timber-framed Underbank Hall, situated on

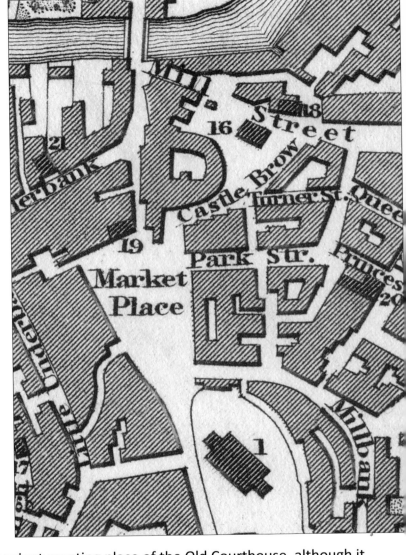

Above: 5.13 The Market Place in 1824, an open space cleared of its old buildings

84

Great Underbank below the Market Place, was bought by public subscription with the intention of converting it into a town hall. In the following year, however, a new site was provided for such a building and Underbank Hall instead became a bank, a role which continues to this day.[25]

In 1824 the inhabitants of the Market Place, with the help of the surveyor of the highways, raised £500 to buy the old buildings at the east end of the Market Place from Lady Warren Bulkeley, the lady of the manor. They were then demolished, leaving the Market Place as an open space and providing an uninterrupted view to the newly rebuilt parish church (5.13).[26] The old permanent shambles were now replaced by wooden booths, which could be moved or cleared away as required.[27] In the same year a new Meal and Cheese House was built on land given by Lady Warren Bulkeley at the corner of the present Vernon Street and Warren Street (5.14).

Above: 5.14 The Meal and Cheese House on Vernon Street, built in 1824. This building and its later extensions once served as the town hall.

The ground floor contained the cheese and meal markets, while the upper floor became the venue for meetings of the manorial court and other official business. James Butterworth in 1827 described it as the place in which 'the chief affairs belonging to the town are settled. The justice meetings held and all public discussions on subjects connected with parochial affairs transacted'.[28] This new building, to which extensions were later added, effectively remained Stockport's town hall until the present building was built on Wellington Road South in 1904-8.

The New Market on Hillgate

In addition to the improvements to the Market Place, there was also an attempt to set up a second market in the town. This 'New Market' was built in 1830-1, on a plot of land behind the Old Admiral public house on Middle Hillgate within the heart of Hillgate's substantial industrial community, and consisted of twenty small one-roomed shops set along two sides of a courtyard (5.15-5.17). The market was intended for the sale of meat, fish and vegetables,

Above: 5.15 The New Market on Ordnance Survey mapping of 1849
Below: 5.16 The Old Admiral and the entrance to the New Market

and its brick-built shops, which could be locked up at night, offered accommodation superior to the wooden stalls and booths of the Market Place.[29] The New Market also seems to have been built on private land but to have been established with the support of John Kenyon Winterbottom, who was the steward of the manor and in 1831 and 1832 was elected Stockport's mayor.[30] In 1835 the manorial court recommended that the potato market should be held there.[31] A market was still operating here in the early 1840s, but by this stage the manorial authorities were seeking to have it closed down. One of the landowners, James Newton, responded by trying to sell his share of the property to the manor but without success.[32] In January 1844 a temporary indoor circus was built in the New Market's courtyard, in which evening performances were staged by gaslight.[33] The former market stalls were later used for a variety of other purposes, such as stores, stables, a smithy and a butcher's slaughterhouse.[34]

Fairs and Early Balloonists

The growth of Stockport's population also had an impact on its annual fairs. These continued to be used by farmers and traders for the sale of livestock, with the May event being singled out in 1810 as 'a considerable cattle-fair'.[35] The May and October fairs were also pleasure fairs. During those times, two days, the 1st of May and the 23rd of October, were given as holidays by most of the town's factory owners.[36] The May fair appears to have been the greater and during the nineteenth century the *Stockport Advertiser* regularly reported its proceedings. The town was decked out for the occasion, and May Day began with the arrival of milk delivery boys from the surrounding countryside, their carts, horses and themselves festooned with garlands and ribbons.

The May fair also brought circus troops, travelling menageries, waxworks, sideshows and other fairground attractions. These entertainments were originally centred on the Market Place. The available space was increased in 1824 by the removal of the shambles and the old Meal and Cheese House, the site of which came to be regularly occupied by a travelling menagerie

Above: 5.17 The New Market street sign, reinstated at the market site

amongst other shows.[37] A second venue arose from the partial infilling of the valley of the Hempshaw Brook on the south side of the town. Here, on glebe land, material was dumped from the demolition and rebuilding of the parish church, the widening of Churchgate, and finally the construction of the new Wellington Road. On the resulting newly made ground, Waterloo Road was built and from about 1826 this area was used as an overspill for the fair.[38] Congestion in the Market Place during the May fair was such that traffic could barely negotiate the turnpike route which ran along the north side between Churchgate and Park Street. The west side of the Market Place was used for larger sideshows, positioned facing the shops at this end and, as a result, a source of nuisance to the shopkeepers.[39]

In the late 1820s the courtyard of Castle Mill was the scene of another visiting attraction when balloonists set off from here on display flights (5.18). The first ascent was made on the 18th of June 1827 to mark the twelfth anniversary of the battle of Waterloo. The aeronaut Charles Green was well known for his balloon ascents in the towns of the region and on this occasion was accompanied by a passenger, Mr Gee of Edgeley. For a charge of 2s 6d spectators were allowed to enter Castle Yard to witness the launch and for an additional 1 shilling could view the proceedings from the greater comfort of the Castle Inn. Relatively few paid admittance but, according to the *Stockport Advertiser*, the crowd which gathered outside was the largest in living memory, as people packed the Market Place and surrounding streets, while others watched from the tops of

ROYAL BALLOON, 75TH ASCENT,

Under the Patronage of HENRY HODGKINSON, Esq. THE MAYOR.

MR GREEN most respectfully announces to the Nobility and Gentry of this Vicinity, that at the request of many of his Friends in this town, he purposes to make a Second Ascent from the *Castle Yard*, on MONDAY next, and in order that it may not interfere with the business of the day, the Ascent will take place at FIVE o'clock in the afternoon.

Tickets of Amission to witness the inflation and Ascent in the *Castle Yard*, *One Shilling and Sixpence* each, and for the accommodation of select Visitors, (more particularly Ladies,) Rooms in the Castle Inn, will be fitted up with seats commanding the most eligible view, Admission to which, will be *One Shilling* extra.

Tickets to be had at the *Advertiser-Office*, of Mr CLAYE, Bookseller, at the *Castle Inn*, at the *Warren-Bulkeley Arms Inn*, and of Mr LARKUM, at the *Gas Works*, Stockport.

Above: 5.18 Announcing Stockport's second balloon ascent on the 8th of July 1827

houses and even the church tower. Charles Green and his son made a second ascent three weeks later when the admittance charge was reduced to 1s 6d, including 6d worth of refreshments, the ascent was scheduled for later in the day, and there was a much larger number of paying spectators.[40]

'Some very elegant shops'

'The Market Place is now nearly surrounded by some very elegant shops' wrote James Butterworth in 1827 and his statement is borne out by contemporary trade directories. They show that by the 1820 and 1830s trade was being carried out from virtually all the properties on the south, west and east sides of the Market Place (see Appendix).[41] Among these there were eight public houses, which included the now defunct Rose and Crown, Sun, Angel, and Castle Inn, as well as the Pack Horse, Bull's Head, Boar's Head (5.19) and the George and Dragon, later rebuilt as the Baker's Vaults.[42] Three properties were occupied by dealers in the traditional staples of the town's trade, corn and cheese. There was also a single butcher's shop, but for the most part the goods sold in the shops around the Market Place differed from the perishable foodstuffs and general provisions sold in the market and were more exclusive. By far the largest group of traders were the drapers, who can be identified at no fewer than ten shops, more than a quarter of the total premises, followed by seven or so grocers' shops. Both groups were among the elite of Stockport's shopkeepers, catering for the better-off customer.[43] In 1825 two-fifths of the town's drapers were to be found on the Market Place, and from about this period the more

Above: 5.19 The Boar's Head, an early nineteenth-century public house

SUMMER FASHIONS.

W. WEBB, MARKET PLACE, STOCKPORT,

RESPECTFULLY announces to his Friends and the Inhabitants of Stockport and neighbourhood, that he h. RETURNED FROM LONDON with a FASHIONABLE STOCK OF GOODS for the approaching Season, which a NOW READY for inspection.

Stockport, April 26th, 1843.

SUMMER FASHIONS.

G. DRIKWATER

RESPECTFULLY announces his return from London, and that HIS SHOW ROOMS ARE NOW OPEN wi. A FASHIONABLE AND EXTENSIVE STOCK OF GOODS, adapted for the present Season.

IN BONNETS, Leghorn, Rutland, Dunstable, Bedford, Rice, Tuscan, Satin China, Princess Royal, Brilliants, Honeycomb, a Brussels Tuscans, and a choice assortment of Paris and Swiss Fancies, Ladies and Children's Col'd drawn Batiste and other fan Bonnet Materials.

AN EXTENSIVE AND SPLENDID ASSORTMENT OF FRENCH AND BRITISH RIBBONS, FLOWERS, PLAI AND FANCY PARASOLS, IN GREAT VARIETY.

FOR DRESSES, Plain and Brocaded Gros, Satinetts, Ottomans, Barathes, Fancy Muslins, Balzarines, Pekin-Crapes, Mouselin de-laines, Cashmeres, &c., &c.

FOREIGN AMD BRITISH SHAWLS, SCARFS, HANDKERCHIEFS, &c., In Norwich, Ottoman, Scotch, Cashmere, pla and figured Satins, L'amas, and a variety of other Fancy Kinds.

British and Foreign Lace, Muslin and Cambric Collars, Habit Shirts, Cuffs, Gloves, London Stays, &c.

G. D. invites attention to his Stock of West of England and Yorkshire BROAD CLOTHS, in all colors.—The variety of Fan. Trouserings and Vestings of different materials, suitable for the Season, is immense.

Market Place, Stockport, April 28th, 1843.

prestigious of these regularly announced the arrival of the latest fashions from London (5.20). By contrast, it was estimated in 1833 that half of the town's population bought clothing from travelling salesmen, often agents of firms based in Manchester, for which payment was made by instalments.[44] The single greatest concentration of drapers and grocers lay on the north side of the Market Place. Here, along with a hosier, they occupied all but one of the properties between Park Street and Millgate.

William Shuttleworth's painting of about 1810 shows the north and south sides of the Market Place lined with a mixture of three-storey brick Georgian buildings and earlier two-storey structures whose gabled facades betrayed their timber-framed origins (5.21). A number of ground-floor shop fronts are in evidence, some inserted into earlier buildings. The appearance of one property at this time was deceptive. In about 1785 Staircase House was divided into two parts, of which No 30 was leased to the first of a succession of drapers, while No 31 was occupied as a grocer's and candle manufacturer's.[45] At about the same time the timber-framed

Above: 5.20 Announcing the latest fashions in 1843

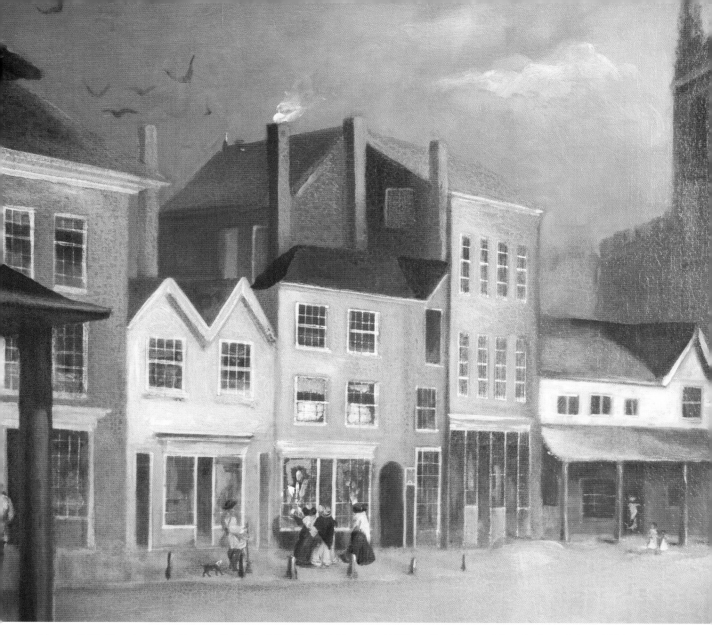

Above: 5.21 The shops on the north side of the Market Place on William Shuttleworth's painting of circa 1810. The building in the centre is Staircase House.

facade was replaced by a new brick frontage. At No 30 this not only masked the old gabled roofline and but also included windows painted onto the brickwork to give the illusion of a third storey. Neighbouring timber-framed buildings on this side of the Market Place were replaced in brick within a few years of Shuttleworth's painting.[46] It is likely that many of the brick buildings on the Market Place at the time of the painting had themselves been erected within the previous two or three decades. Among the largest of the Georgian additions to the Market Place was the present No 28 which by the 1790s was owned and occupied by the corn factor Bradford Norbury (5.22).[47] It stands at the corner with Park Street, which was described as 'new' in 1785 and was laid out as part of the development of the former agricultural land on the north side of the Market Place.[48] No 25 & 27 Market Place, on the opposite corner with Park Street, is probably of a similar date (5.23).

Above: 5.22 The former town house of the corn factor Bradford Norbury (now Blackshaw's Cafe). This building was attacked by rioters in 1795. Below: 5.23 No 26 & 27 Market Place, a late eighteenth-century building

Rebuilding the Parish Church

By the late eighteenth century the ancient fabric of Stockport's parish church of St Mary, built of the soft local sandstone, was in an advanced state of decay. The tower, already in a dangerous condition, is said to have been further damaged in 1805 when the church bells were rung for three days in celebration of Nelson's victory at Trafalgar. By 1810, for safety reasons, the nave

Above: 5.24 St Mary's Church after the rebuilding of the nave and tower in 1813-17

could no longer be used by worshippers.[49] In that year demolition began, leaving only the medieval chancel standing. On the 5th of July 1813 the foundation stone of the new church was laid, and work was completed four years later (5.24, 5.25). The new building, comprising a nave and western tower, was designed by the architect Lewis Wyatt. His commissions were usually for country houses but his work at St Mary's is judged to demonstrate a knowledge of Gothic architecture equal to that of any of his contemporaries. Wyatt also designed the stone screen which frames the entrance to the churchyard from the Market Place. The church tower was provided with new bells in 1817, cast by the bell-founder John Rudhall of Gloucester (5.26).

Above: 5.25 St Mary's Church, looking along the nave to the tower

To pay for the rebuilding, successive Acts of Parliament in 1810 and 1815 allowed a rate to be levied on all occupants of property in the parish, despite opposition from Stockport's nonconformists who included some of the town's leading industrialists. The funding of the rebuilding was still a contentious issue as late as 1833 when ratepayers, having contributed £32,000, were asked to pay off an outstanding debt of over £7000. In the following year the matter ended in a compromise under which half of this money was provided by private donations.[50] The chancel was restored in 1848 and the church underwent further alterations in 1881-2, which included the addition of the west window in the tower and the insertion of the great arch between the tower and the nave.[51]

Above: 5.26 Bells of Saint Mary's Church, cast in 1817

Above: 5.27 'The Cheshire Farmer', arriving at the foot of Mealhouse Brow

Riots, Radicals and Reactionaries

In 1784 Jonathan Thatcher, a farmer at Woodbank on the east side of the town, showed his opposition to a tax on saddle horses by riding his cow to and from the market. The incident became the subject of a caricature showing Thatcher, 'The Cheshire Farmer', arriving at the Sun Inn at the foot of Mealhouse Brow (5.27). Copies were even circulated in Parliament, with one reputedly reaching prime minister Pitt.[52]

For all its celebrity, Thatcher's protest was a fairly trivial incident. A far more serious matter were the periods of social unrest and political radicalism which accompanied the growth of Stockport as an industrial town and which at times erupted into violent confrontations between the forces of authority and the lower classes.

In the 1790s there were food riots in the Market Place. Stockport was one of several Cheshire towns where there was rioting in 1795 as a result of rising corn prices. The focus of the crowd's anger was Bradford Norbury whose house on the corner of Park Street was pelted with stones. Norbury was a prominent figure among the town's corn factors, the middlemen who bought corn from farmers and were seen as profiteering at the cost of the poor.[53] There was rioting again in the Market Place in 1799 when a crowd seized carts bringing meal and flour for sale, and shops were attacked. In January of the following year a local magistrate, fearing more trouble, asked farmers to bring corn, meal and flour to the market and to sell it not to middlemen but 'there retail to the poor at a reasonable profit'.[54]

Reactionary forces, who opposed the demands of radicals for political change, used the Market Place for their own forms of demonstration. In December 1792, after a royal proclamation outlawed seditious literature, a crowd in the Market Place burnt an effigy of the author Thomas Paine, whose *Rights of Man* had defended the French Revolution.[55] Radical societies existed in Stockport in the 1790s and 1800s but, despite the fears of the authorities, their membership was limited to only a tiny minority of the local population. Demands for political change first received mass support in Stockport and elsewhere within the region in about 1816. Handloom weavers, faced with a shortage of work and falling wages, petitioned the government for assistance. When their voice was ignored, they increasingly looked for a solution in the reform of Parliament itself. The campaign was at its strongest in 1819, but on the 16th of August that year a great radical meeting at St Peter's Fields in Manchester was broken up by mounted troops resulting in deaths and injuries. In the crowd on that day was a contingent of perhaps 1400-1500 people from Stockport. Peterloo, as the event came to be known, was the culmination of a series of mass gatherings held that year, which included meetings held in Stockport at Sandy Brow on the fringe of the town. At the first of these, in February 1819, a 'cap of liberty', a symbol of revolution, was raised. When the Stockport Yeomanry and special constables moved in to break up the meeting, they were forced back by the crowd, and the episode became a cause of celebration among radicals in the region and was even commemorated in verse. The Stockport yeomanry, which was a volunteer troop of cavalry said to consist mostly of local farmers, later took part in the dispersal of the Peterloo meeting and viewed the occasion as a chance to avenge their humiliation at Sandy Brow. One member of the yeomanry seized banners from the crowd and these were later burnt in the Market Place.[56]

Castle Mill, overlooking the Market Place, proved a boon to the authorities. In 1779 cannon had been mounted here to deter an anticipated attack by Lancashire textile workers. The mill was commandeered in 1817 when the marchers known as the Blanketeers, after the blankets which they carried for the journey, left Manchester for London to petition for Parliamentary reform. Most were halted at Stockport, others at Macclesfield, and a total of about two hundred were temporarily detained within the yard of Castle Mill.[57]

The site on the Market Place most closely associated with successive radical movements was the Bull's Head (5.28). In January 1819, a month before the first meeting at Sandy Brow, Henry 'Orator' Hunt, who was later arrested at Peterloo, addressed a crowd in the Market Place from a window of the Bull's Head.[58] In 1838 the Bull's Head was also the local venue for meetings of the Chartist movement. In an echo of 1819, crowds in the Market Place were addressed from a first-floor window of the inn by speakers who included Feargus O'Connor and Joseph Rayner Stephens, two of the movement's leading figures.[59]

Above: 5.28 The Bull's Head, a venue for radical and Chartist meetings

6. An Age of Improvements, 1840-1912

The period from about 1840 until the early twentieth century was one of mixed fortunes for Stockport. In the late 1830s and early 1840s the town was hit especially hard by a major slump in the cotton industry.[1] A number of mills closed, others went on short time, and houses fell empty as their occupants either left the town, some for a new life overseas, or moved into shared accommodation to save money. On the doors of vacated properties were the words 'Stockport to let'. This was also the time that the railway arrived in the town. A link with Manchester opened in 1840 and in 1842 a great new viaduct carried its first services across the Mersey valley.

For three decades after this slump the town experienced a period of stagnation in which the total population hardly grew. This period was punctuated by a series of further downturns in the cotton industry, including the Cotton Famine of 1861-5. In 1852 it also saw tensions against Irish immigrants erupt into rioting which left one person dead and the town's two Catholic churches ransacked.

In the 1880s the fortunes of the town entered a new era. Its ailing cotton industry was revived by the construction of massive new mills. Other local industries were expanding. Hatting had already begun a process of mechanization, led by the Stockport firm of Christys. Engineering, previously of minor local significance, now developed into a major employer and was of particular importance in the new industrial suburb of Reddish. As a result of its broader industrial base, Stockport was better placed than many other towns in the region to weather the final decline of the cotton industry in the twentieth century.

The status of the town also changed. In 1889 the municipal borough of Stockport, created over fifty years earlier, became a county borough, largely independent from the control of the new Cheshire County Council. Boundary changes in 1901 and 1911 more than doubled the size of the borough and increased its population to about 120,000.

Facing page: 6.1 Stockport market, about 1910

The Market and the Manor

The creation in 1835 of the municipal borough with an elected town council did not mean the end of manorial authority and for a number of years the two continued to operate side by side. The relationship was not an easy one. An early sign of the problems to come with regard to the market occurred in 1837 when the council appointed its own 'market lookers' to regulate the quality of meat and fish. Undeterred, the court leet continued to elect its own officials for these duties.[2] In 1840 the right to collect the tolls of Stockport's market and fairs, which had been previously leased out, passed back into the manorial hands.[3] The lord of the manor at this period was George John Warren, the fifth Lord Vernon (6.2). His ancestral seat was at Sudbury Hall in Derbyshire but from the late 1830s he spent most of his life in Italy. His reclaiming of the manorial tolls occurred at a period when the market was in difficulty. The arrival of the railway quickly resulted in a weekly flow of shoppers from Stockport to Manchester, returning with a range of goods from clothing to greengroceries.[4] The economic slump of this period meant that for many there was little money to spend. In August 1842 Stockport's Friday market was 'meagrely supplied and very thinly attended by both country people and buyers'. The same year the landlord of the Bull's Head reported that the inn used to be filled with factory workers on a Saturday night 'so that you could hardly get a seat; now the number of those who come is comparatively very small indeed'. Traders who had previously rented a stall at the market or fair might now be found hawking their goods from a basket.[5]

In 1841 Lord Vernon and his steward, Thomas Ashworth, began to change the way the market operated. The first step was the demolition of the old Castle Mill at the Market Place's northwest corner. Since ceasing to be used first as a cotton factory and then as a muslin hall, Castle

Above: 6.2 George John Warren, the fifth Lord Vernon (1803-66), until 1850 lord of the manor of Stockport

Mill had become a storage space for stall holders while its front part continued as the Castle Inn.[6] The demolition of the building and levelling of the site significantly extended the market area. In the same year Ashworth had a number of small iron markers inscribed 'Manor Market' set into the ground in the Market Place and the streets leading into it, thereby defining the area in which trading could take place, and in which tolls could be collected.[7] Market trading outside the prescribed area was prohibited (6.3). They were part of a number of manorial markers set up at this period. Others, in the form of cast-iron posts, were placed all along the manor boundary (6.4).

Left: 6.3 The manorial steward tightens control over the market, 1841
Above: 6.4 A manorial boundary post on Portwood Bridge

STOCKPORT
FAIRS & MARKETS.
NOTICE.

LORD VERNON, as Lord of the Manor of **STOCKPORT**, being exclusively entitled to the Fairs and Markets within the same Manor. and having, in order to afford accommodation to Persons frequenting the said Fairs and Markets, caused the Castle Inn and Premises to be taken down, and the Ground added to the Old Market Place,

NOTICE IS HEREBY GIVEN,

That all Persons attending the said Fairs and Markets with Horses, Cattle, Goods, Wares, Merchandise, and other Matters, are henceforth to expose to Sale, and place the same, in the public Market Place, and in the other places set apart by the Lord of the Manor for the holding of the Fairs and Markets therein, and not on or in any Lands, Grounds, or places belonging to other Individuals, to the injury of the rights of the *Manor.--Dated this Fifteenth day of April,* 1841.

THOMAS ASHWORTH,
STEWARD.

PRINTED BY T. M. KING, BRIDGE-STREET, STOCKPORT.

In 1842 Ashworth had a new list of tolls printed, reiterating the existing charges, and a board showing the tolls was set up in the Court House. He also had the regulations of the market put on display (6.5).[8] Many of the clauses stipulated where different goods and produce were to be sold, and these were a mixture of new and old arrangements. As before, cheese and meal were to be sold at the Court House on Warren Street. The butchers' shambles were to be located on the north side of the Market Place, the stalls for potatoes on the east side, and the stalls for fish on the south side. Castle Yard, the former site of Castle Mill, was now to be used for the sale of cattle and pigs.[9]

Lord Vernon's Market House

By May 1842 Lord Vernon had commissioned the building of a new Market House on the west side of the Market Place, next to the site

Right: 6.5 'Orders and Regulations' of the market, 1842

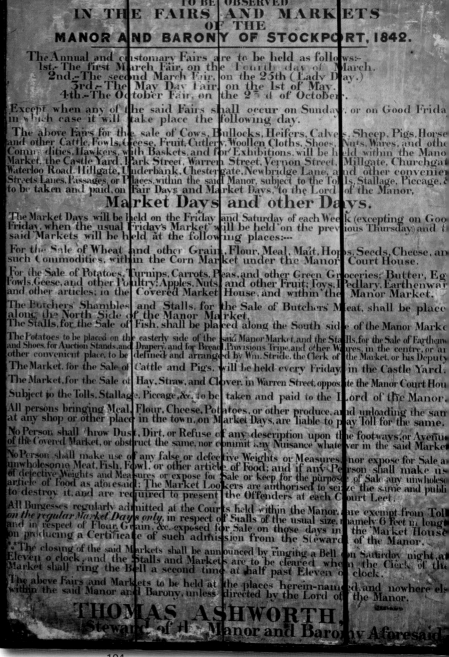

ORDERS AND REGULATIONS
TO BE OBSERVED
IN THE FAIRS AND MARKETS
OF THE
MANOR AND BARONY OF STOCKPORT, 1842.

The Annual and customary Fairs are to be held as follows:-
1st.- The first March Fair, on the Fourth day of March.
2nd.- The second March Fair, on the 25th (Lady Day.)
3rd.- The May Day Fair, on the 1st of May.
4th.- The October Fair, on the 23d of October.

Except when any of the said Fairs shall occur on Sunday, or on Good Friday in which case it will take place the following day.

The above Fairs for the sale of Cows, Bullocks, Heifers, Calves, Sheep, Pigs, Horses and other Cattle, Fowls, Geese, Fruit, Cutlery, Woollen Cloths, Shoes, Nuts, Wares, and other Commodities, Hawkers, with Baskets, and for Exhibitions, will be held within the Manor Market, the Castle Yard, Park Street, Warren Street, Vernon Street, Millgate, Churchgate, Waterloo Road, Hillgate, Underbank, Chestergate, Newbridge Lane, and other convenient Streets, Lanes, Passages, or Places, within the said Manor, subject to the Tolls, Stallage, Piccage, &c. to be taken and paid, on Fair Days and Market Days, to the Lord of the Manor.

Market Days and other Days.

The Market Days will be held on the Friday and Saturday of each Week (excepting on Good Friday, when the usual Friday's Market will be held on the previous Thursday) and the said Markets will be held at the following places:---

For the Sale of Wheat and other Grain, Flour, Meal, Malt, Hops, Seeds, Cheese, and such Commodities, within the Corn Market under the Manor Court House.

For the Sale of Potatoes, Turnips, Carrots, Peas, and other Green Groceries; Butter, Eggs, Fowls, Geese, and other Poultry; Apples, Nuts, and other Fruit; Toys, Pedlary, Earthenware, and other articles; in the Covered Market House, and within the Manor Market.

The Butchers' Shambles and Stalls, for the Sale of Butchers' Meat, shall be placed along the North Side of the Manor Market.

The Stalls, for the Sale of Fish, shall be placed along the South side of the Manor Market.

The Potatoes to be placed on the easterly side of the said Manor Market, and the Stalls, for the Sale of Earthenware and Shoes, for Auction Stands, and Drapery, and for Bread, Provisions, Tripe, and other Wares, in the centre, or at any other convenient place, to be defined and arranged by Wm. Stride, the Clerk of the Market, or his Deputy.

The Market, for the Sale of Cattle and Pigs, will be held every Friday, in the Castle Yard.

The Market, for the Sale of Hay, Straw, and Clover, in Warren Street, opposite the Manor Court House.

Subject to the Tolls, Stallage, Piccage, &c. to be taken and paid to the Lord of the Manor.

All persons bringing Meal, Flour, Cheese, Potatoes, or other produce, and unloading the same at any shop or other place in the town, on Market Days, are liable to pay Toll for the same.

No Person shall throw Dust, Dirt, or Refuse of any description upon the footways, or Avenues of the Covered Market, or obstruct the same, nor commit any Nuisance whatever in the said Market.

No Person shall make use of any false or defective Weights or Measures, nor expose for Sale any unwholesome Meat, Fish, Fowl, or other article of Food; and if any Person shall make use of defective Weights and Measures or expose for Sale or keep for the purpose of Sale any unwholesome article of Food as aforesaid; The Market Lookers are authorised to seize the same and publicly to destroy it, and are required to present the Offenders at each Court Leet.

All Burgesses regularly admitted at the Courts held within the Manor, are exempt from Toll on the regular Market Days only, in respect of Stalls of the usual size, namely 6 feet in length, and in respect of Flour, Grain, &c. exposed for Sale on those days in the Market House, on producing a Certificate of such admission from the Steward of the Manor.

** The closing of the said Markets shall be announced by ringing a Bell on Saturday night at Eleven o'clock, and the Stalls and Markets are to be cleared when the Clerk of the Market shall ring the Bell a second time at half past Eleven o'clock.

The above Fairs and Markets to be held at the places herein-named, and nowhere else within the said Manor and Barony, unless directed by the Lord of the Manor.

THOMAS ASHWORTH,
Steward of the Manor and Barony Aforesaid.

of the former colonnaded seventeenth-century building. He also planned to build new butchers' shambles of brick in place of the current wooden booths. The borough council objected to the new scheme on the grounds that, when required, the wooden booths could be removed from the Market Place to leave an open square for 'elections, processions, public meetings and other public purposes'.[10] The brick shambles were put

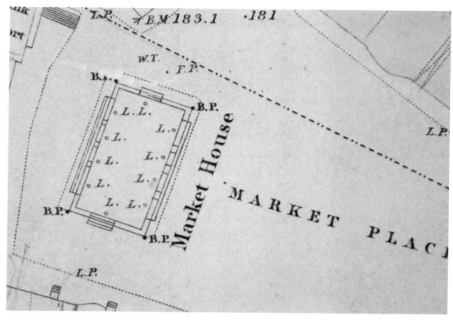

on hold but work on the Market House was soon completed. It is said to have been built 'for the use of the green-grocers and the farmers'.[11] The building was short-lived and no photograph or other illustration is known to have survived. When its construction was announced, the plan was for a brick structure surmounted by a cupola and enclosed so that it could be locked up, but there was evidently some change to the design. In 1844 stall holders within the Market House requested that the lower parts of the sides be enclosed and the upper parts be fitted with shutters, as the building was cold and drafty, and the lack of security meant that goods could not be left there overnight. 'As it now is, the Market House is a place of resort for children and adult persons who commit great nuisances'.[12] It is uncertain whether this request was met. Mapping of 1849 shows that the building measured about 18m by 10m and had entrances on the north and south, with windows or possibly further entrances making up most of the other two sides (6.6). The interior was lit by gaslights. Outside, a boundary post was situated at each corner, presumably in connection with the regulation of the market and collection of tolls. Later critics condemned the building as an eyesore. The mayor, at the laying of the foundation stone of the council's own new Market Hall in 1851, claimed that 'a more unsightly piece of deformity, and a place more unfit for the purpose for which it was intended, could hardly be conceived'.[13]

Above: 6.6 Lord Vernon's short-lived Market House, on Ordnance Survey mapping of 1849

The Toll Collectors called to Account

In 1843 the manorial management of the market was again challenged. Under the stewardship of Thomas Ashworth the tolls were collected by William Stride and George Cooke, who wore a brass plate on their arm as a badge of office (6.7). In the early 1840s the revenues from the market and fairs were reported to be on the increase, but it is unclear as to how much of this was due to Stockport's emergence from recession and how much to the actions of these men.[14]

From about the time of the May fair in 1842 the tolls are said to have been collected with greater severity. The matter came to a head in late May the following year when the borough magistrates' court heard a catalogue of complaints against the toll collectors. For perhaps four decades the manorial authorities had claimed the right to exact tolls on produce being delivered to the town on market days but the toll collectors were now operating with free licence. John Wood, a farmer from Ringway, had come to a Stockport inn on a non-market day to meet a customer from Haughton Green and hand over a delivery of six sacks of flour, when Cooke demanded and exacted a toll of 2 shillings. Another farmer who on market day had shown a buyer a sample sack of potatoes and promised to supply him with 60 loads of the same was promptly charged a toll on that full amount. A carrier delivering malt to the Sun Inn on the Market Place had been threatened with seizure of his horse and cart if he refused to pay toll. For a number of years there had been variations in stallage collected at the fair but there was now a system of demanding double the authorized amount. When John Webb, a Portwood shopkeeper who also rented a stall at the May fair, was charged double by Stride he complained to the steward Thomas Ashworth. He apologized and returned the excess money, but on the following day Stride again demanded double payment and seized some of Webb's stock. Hawkers were also viewed as fair game, and in one case a person selling braces had been followed from pub to pub and made to pay a toll.[15]

Summonses were issued to William Stride and George Cooke for extortion against John Wood and John Webb but when the magistrates referred the cases to the county court at Chester they

Above: 6.7 In the 1840s the manorial toll collectors wore a brass arm badge

were thrown out by the grand jury before coming to trial. Following these proceedings, many of the toll collectors' previous practices were discontinued.[16] However, a few years later George Cooke was unable to list the exemption rights of burgesses, suggesting that the collection was still not being carried out strictly by the book.[17]

The Failed Shambles

In September 1843 the scheme for the new shambles was revived on a grand scale. The *Stockport Advertiser* now announced that work was imminent on the construction of 'a commodious market hall for flesh and fish. It will connect itself with the east end of that already built, extending about 38 feet [11.5m] by 40 feet [12.1m] wide and 19 feet [5.7m] high. The form we understand will be quadrangular, the interior being approached by 16 or 18 entrances of an ornamental character'.[18] The work may have been encouraged by a petition in April of that year signed by 67 Stockport butchers asking for shambles to be built which could be locked at night and provide better protection from the weather.[19]

When the council heard that the scheme was to go ahead, the town clerk Henry Coppock wrote a letter to Edward White, Lord Vernon's representative in London, expressing their opposition and adding that 'It is thought that Lord Vernon were he accessible would not permit this Square to be at all encroached upon but his absence from England prevents his being referred to'. Within days, work began on lifting up the Market Place pavement to prepare the site but was stopped by the borough police. The following week Lord Vernon's men arrived in greater force in the early hours of the morning, erected a fence around the site and again began to lift the paving. They threatened to call in miners from Lord Vernon's Poynton collieries if they met with resistance but were again removed by the police. The immediate tensions seem to have been reduced by a visit by Henry Coppock to Edward White in London, and a reciprocal visit to Stockport. In the longer term, the council, armed with legal advice, decided to continue its opposition and the proposed shambles were never built.[20]

The Corporation's 'Town Castle'

In a speech at the Mayor's Dinner in December 1844 the town clerk Henry Coppock revealed that negotiations had been taking place with Lord Vernon's representatives, and that 'The dawn of better days are now appearing'. An agreement had been reached whereby the Corporation and the lord of the manor would exchange properties to each other's benefit. The council would receive Castle Yard and the Court House on Vernon Street, a building for which they had been paying Lord Vernon a rent of £75 a year. He would now replace this with a freehold rent of only £50, and would lease back the cheese house on the ground floor of the building for the nominal sum of £5. In return the council would transfer to Lord Vernon the old Stockport workhouse at Daw Bank.[21] After three decades of use, this had closed in 1842 when a new larger workhouse, later St Thomas' Hospital, opened at Shaw Heath. The value of the building to Lord Vernon lay in its proximity to the railway, and once it was in his hands it was converted into a coal depot.[22]

The negotiations of 1844 also addressed the contentious issue of the market. Here the council received an undertaking that a 'new cheese house, and butter and egg market' would be built at Lord Vernon's expense. It was to stand on the site of existing buildings which he owned on the west side of the Market Place, and presumably would have replaced his much detested Market Hall, completed only two years before. For their part, the council would construct a new town hall on Castle Yard, to be named the 'Castle' after the early history of the site and to be built in a similar style to the proposed new market hall. Adjacent buildings on Bridge Street Brow were to be pulled down to make way for the town hall entrance. As Henry Coppock explained, 'The burgesses will now have a building for all public purposes, for the due administration of justice consistent with the high character and respectability of Stockport'.[23] The overall scheme, if carried out, would have provided the Market Place with twin public buildings framing Bridge Street Brow. It was not to be. The transfer of the Court House and Castle Yard was completed in May 1845, but the previous month the council had been informed that Lord Vernon would very likely be willing to sell the manorial rights.[24] The Corporation's resources were now channelled in this new direction and the town hall on Castle Yard was never realised, although some still cherished the idea. At the celebratory dinner for the council's own new Market Hall, in September 1851, one of the toasts was 'Success to the New Market Hall, and may it be the prelude to a New Town Castle at an early period'.[25]

The Corporation Buys the Market Rights

In 1847, two years after the council began negotiations to buy the manorial rights, Parliament gave its consent to this transaction in the Stockport Manorial Tolls and Bridges Act. Under its provisions, for an agreed sum of £22,500 the council would assume the manorial rights and acquire property in the Market Place. It would also take over from Lord Vernon an area of farm-land on the east side of the town, known as Stringer's Fields, for use as a public park.[26] The bill met with local opposition which questioned whether the sale was justifiable by the profits arising from the manorial tolls. This controversy is said to have been the major cause of the Tories' success in the local election of November 1848, when they gained a majority of seats on the town council. In August of the following year, however, a special committee reported to the council that it was honour-bound to fulfil the agreement with Lord Vernon.[27] On the 26th of June 1850 the purchase was completed. New, lower, market tolls were introduced which now became the responsibility of a new council body. There was not an entire break with tradition, for the name chosen was the Manorial Tolls Committee.[28] The court leet, which also passed under council control, continued to function in an increasingly ceremonial role until its demise in 1858.[29]

The New Market Hall

For the council in 1850 the creation of the borough's new park was not a priority and it was not until September 1858 that Vernon Park, as it was named, was officially opened. The improvement of the Market Place was more pressing. A timber-framed building once used as a post office and the adjoining house, occupied by the toll collector William Stride, had been included within the purchase and almost immediately were demolished.[30] These properties, along with a neighbouring building occupied by the Bank of Stockport, had been proposed for the site of Lord Vernon's new market building in 1844. Instead, in 1851-2 the council built its own Market Hall here, also later known as the Produce Hall or Hen Market. The architects Stevens and Park of Macclesfield designed the

Above: 6.8 The Corporation's new Market Hall, 1852

building, which was built at a cost of £4000. It was constructed with an ornate stone classical facade, with a balcony at first-floor level (6.8). This feature was specifically designed for electioneering purposes, from which speakers could address an audience in the Market Place below. The facade of the building was deceptive. It gave the impression that the interior contained both a ground and first floor but, as originally designed, it was open to an arched iron roof. The building also contained a basement with storerooms which could be leased to traders. The cost of the stone facade was a cause of argument within the council but was viewed by its supporters as a matter of civic pride, and the laying of the foundation stone on the 17th of September 1851 was marked with a procession and speeches by civic dignitaries, followed in the evening by a celebratory dinner in a local inn. In May 1852 the council also approved the addition of a fish market to the building, again designed by Stevens and Park.[31]

Above: 6.9 The Market Place in 1859, an open space once more

In the mid 1870s an upper floor was inserted within the Market Hall which now became the location of the town's public library, transferred here from Vernon Park Museum. The new premises were more centrally placed but it is said that at this period the ground floor contained the cheese market and that the smell rising to the library was at times overpowering until the building's ventilation was sufficiently improved.[32] In 1913 the library moved again, to a new building erected on the corner of St Petersgate and Wellington Road, the present Stockport Central Library.

Castle Yard and the Cattle Market

In May 1851 the short-lived Market House built by Lord Vernon was taken down, leaving the Market Place once again as an open space (6.9).[33] By this time the council had begun its own reorganization of the market, with the new Market Hall as the focal point, but their relocation of stalls prompted complaints from a number of traders. In 1852 it was agreed to move the potato market from Castle Yard back to its former location by the parish church.[34] In the following year the cattle market was transferred back to Castle Yard from Mersey Street in the Park. In preparation for that move, the yard was partly enclosed by a wall, and railings were added along Vernon Street which was also widened to improve access to the site.[35] It is said that Castle Yard was also reduced in height at this time.[36] Archaeological investigations here in 2003 found evidence for

Above: 6.10 The cattle market in Castle Yard, 1892

the removal of Castle Mill in 1841 and possible levelling in 1853 in the form of a demolition layer containing eighteenth-century brick and other make-up layers, all directly overlying the natural sandstone.[37]

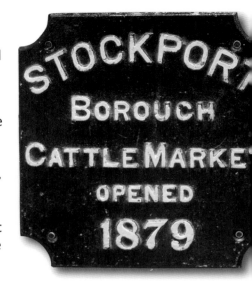

In 1879 a new fairground was established for the sale of cattle on a site on Great Portwood Street in Portwood, adjacent to the council's gasworks (6.11).[38] This site was used for the town's increasing number of cattle fairs but Castle Yard remained the site of a weekly Friday market for cattle, horses, sheep and pigs, and livestock was still being sold here at the turn of the century (6.10, 6.12).[39] To prevent the livestock causing an obstruction, in 1894 the Manorial Tolls Committee instructed that on market days a chain was to be fixed between the Baker's Vaults and the railings on Vernon Street and that cattle were to be kept within this enclosure.[40] It was on the east side of this cattle market that in 1895-6 a new office building for the county borough's weights and measures inspector was built, overlooking Vernon Street (6.13).[41]

Changes at the Court House

The reorganization of the early 1850s also involved the meal and cheese market. Since 1824 this had been housed on the ground floor of the Court House building at the bottom of Vernon Street. Following the creation of the municipal borough, this site increasingly took on an administrative role and less of a commercial one. In 1836 the council received policing

Above: 6.11 A gate plaque from the Portwood cattle fairground
Below: 6.12 'Pig Ellen', a pig seller in Castle Yard, 1888

powers, and an annexe was subsequently added on Vernon Street for the police officers. A fire engine house was built to the rear of the police station in 1842, on a site excavated from the sandstone bedrock of Castle Hill by inmates of the Stockport workhouse. In 1854 the council agreed that the cheese market below the Court House was also to be converted to a fire engine house. The new location for the cheese market was a shop on the Market Place formerly occupied by Henry Whitmore, a draper and tailor.[42] It formed part of a block which once projected into the Market Place from the top of Bridge Street Brow. The site was distinguished by a ground-floor portico, just visible in Shuttleworth's painting of the Market Place in the 1800s (5.3). In 1861, when the Covered Market was constructed, this building and the neighbouring George and Dragon public house of John Baker were demolished, and the pub was rebuilt as the present Baker's Vaults.[43] The Court House itself was extensively renovated in 1878-80 when a second court room was also added.[44]

Above: 6.13 The weights and measures inspectors' office on Castle Yard

The Covered Market Place

By 1860 the butchers, and perhaps other traders, were pressing for the Market Place to be covered, to provide better shelter for themselves and their customers. One correspondent to the *Stockport Advertiser* noted that, in wet weather, the traders' takings were reduced and with them the tolls received by the council. 'Spend your money in improving your market, and the expenditure will probably be covered, very soon by increased tolling'.[45] Less than

a decade had passed since the council had opened up the Market Place by clearing away Lord Vernon's Market House and erecting its own expensive Market Hall, but councillors agreed to the new proposal and in April 1860 advertised for interested contractors to submit designs and costs (6.14). One of the designs included the option of a dome, another of a tower. The Manorial Tolls Committee initially favoured a proposal by Henry Lloyd of Bristol for a structure with sides carried on iron columns, with the space between them filled by cast-iron railings, and with a

Above: 6.14 The council advertises for designs for the Covered Market, April 1860
Right: 6.15 Shudehill Market, Manchester, 1854, the probable inspiration for Stockport's Covered Market

timber roof covered by slates. There were reservations within the council and these seem to have been confirmed by a fact-finding visit to Wolverhampton Market and Shudehill Market in Manchester by a team which included the mayor and borough surveyor. Their conclusion was that Shudehill provided the best model and, as a result, the competition for covering Stockport's Market Place was reopened.[46] The chosen design, judged to be the 'cheapest and the best', was by James Haywood junior, of the Phoenix Foundry and Engineering Works in Derby.[47] The works' previous contracts had included the Shudehill market and the cast-iron roof of the Wolverhampton market, both in 1853-4, and later in the 1860s Haywood would construct the arched roof of Derby's market hall.[48] Shudehill was the largest single market roof in its day and, although much

Above: 6.16 The west end of the Market Place, with the Covered Market (left) and the Produce Hall (right), 1896

grander in scale, it bore many similarities to Haywood's design for Stockport (6.15). It may also have been the Shudehill market which first prompted the idea of covering over Stockport's Market Place. Groundworks for the Covered Market seem to have been under way by February 1861 and by autumn of that year the building was effectively complete, bar the installation of gaslighting.[49]

The Covered Market was built over the central part of the Market Place, leaving a roadway on each side. It also followed the Market Place's triangular plan, so that the building was wider on the west than on the east (6.1, 6.16, 6.17). It was constructed with a roof structure of wrought-iron trusses carried on cast-iron girders, which were in turn supported by cast-iron columns arranged along the sides of the building and in rows within the interior (6.18). Externally the bays, formed by adjacent pairs of columns, were each topped with a gable. The main roof structure ran between the gables in the long side elevations, while gables in the end elevations were intended to give the exterior a more uniform appearance (6.19). Cast-iron finials were set on the gables and carry the date 1861 (6.20). The upper parts of the sides and ends of the building were filled with simple tracery but the lower parts were open. To keep down the cost, the tracery was at first left unglazed but in 1864-5 one bay after another was filled with glass.[50] This offered greater protection from the elements while still allowing access from all sides, and earned the building the nickname of 'the glass umbrella'.[51]

Above: 6.17 The Covered Market, with its lower sides open. It was nicknamed 'the glass umbrella'.
Facing page. Above: 6.18 The roof of the Covered Market. Below: 6.19 The gables at the east end of the Covered Market

117

The roof was clad with timber and slate, except at each apex where it was glazed and louvred to provide ventilation. The supporting columns differed in form. The interior columns were round and narrow. The external columns were square, with those at the corners of the building noticeably wider than the rest, and had decorated capitals. The column at the north-east corner of the building, facing the church, included the name of Haywood (see page vi). The external columns also served as waste pipes, carrying away rainwater from the roof.[52] The interior of the building was flagged with red and blue Staffordshire tiles.[53] The south side of the building crossed the most uneven part of the Market Place, where there was a dip towards the entrance to Mealhouse Brow. Here the ground level was raised to provide an even floor within the building, and externally steps were added to give access to and from the Market Place (6.21).[54] At the time of the building's construction the Market Place was lit by eleven gaslights. In June 1862 these were replaced by new lights fixed to both the external and internal columns of the Covered Market. They were manufactured by a local engineer, Robert Harlow, and were noted for their superior illumination and novel spherical design, which was perhaps inspired by lighting around St George's Hall in Liverpool.[55] The first stalls used within the Covered Market were the old butchers' stalls, modified for the new building.[56]

The Corporation and the Regulation of the Market

In August 1862 the council introduced a series of byelaws for 'the government, regulation, and management' of the market and had these set up on public display (6.22). The byelaws defined the extent of the market and the parts where different produce and goods could be sold. The Covered Market was for butchers, earthenware and hardware dealers, and traders in dry goods and vegetables.

Above: 6.20 A finial on the Covered Market with the date 1861
Right: 6.21 The steps facing Mealhouse Brow. Facing page: 6.22 The Corporation's byelaws for the market, 1862

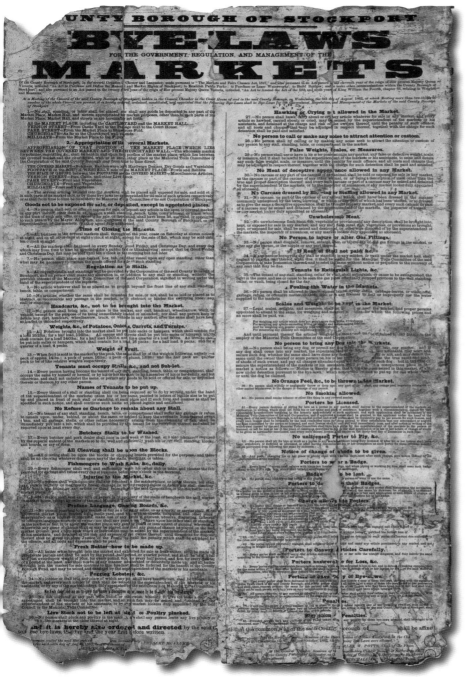

Fowls and rabbits were to be sold on the pavement on the south-west side of the Market Place and 'miscellaneous articles' in the space between the footpaths and the Covered Market. Vernon Street could be used for the sale of pigs, cattle and other livestock. The wholesale market for fruit and vegetables was to be located between the Covered Market and the churchyard. Retail fruit and vegetables could be sold on those parts of Park Street, Millgate and Churchgate nearest to the Market Place. The byelaws also contained extensive provisions about weights and measures, hygiene, litter, the quality of food, and behaviour within the market, including a ban on swearing, games of chance, and smoking in the Covered Market. Traders were not allowed to call out to attract customers and hawking in the market was now prohibited. The byelaws also included detailed regulations about porters, hired to carry a customer's shopping. They had to be licensed, wear a badge to that effect, and could charge no more than the scale of fees which the byelaws laid down (6.23). It was common at this period for councils to follow the opening of a new market hall by issuing market byelaws. It was also typical for those byelaws to seek to give the market a greater air of respectability.[57]

Although the regulations of 1862 defined the area of the market, the old custom continued whereby any provisions and consumable goods brought into the town might be liable for toll. In 1865 the council voted to abolish the practice, which was believed to be of dubious legality, deterred suppliers from coming to the town and often provoked a public row when a payment was demanded.[58]

St Petersgate Bridge

In the 1860s, having covered over the Market Place, the council addressed the question of access. There had been gradual improvements since the creation of Park Street in the late eighteenth century but the steepness of most of the streets leading to the Market Place remained a hindrance (6.24). It was also a factor behind a tragic accident in December 1860. Celebrations were taking place for the laying of the foundation stone of a tower and observatory

Above: 6.23 A market porter's badge. Below: 6.24 Looking up Mealhouse Brow towards the Market Place, about 1920

in Vernon Park, when there was a rush of people from the Market Place down Mealhouse Brow to watch a firework display. Seven people were trampled to death, and others injured.[59]

In 1864 it was decided to build a bridge over Little Underbank to link the Market Place to St Petersgate. This provided a level approach from the west of the town and from the railway station. St Petersgate Bridge was built with five arches of brick, mostly hidden by adjoining buildings, and an iron section spanning Little Underbank (6.25). It was built next to Turner's Steps, an existing pedestrian link between Little Underbank and the Market Place. The bridge was opened in 1868, much to the consternation of shopkeepers in the Underbanks who feared that the new access route to the Market Place would reduce their own passing trade.[60]

To make way for the extension of St Petersgate across the bridge, properties at the south-west corner of the Market Place were demolished. In 1868 a grand new commercial building was erected at the corner of the Market Place and this new road (6.26). It was designed in what was described as a 'Grecian-Italian' style by the Stockport architect T H Allen for the Bank of Stockport

Above: 6.25 Little Underbank and St Petersgate Bridge, about 1905. Below: 6.26 The former Bank of Stockport, built in 1868

(later the Manchester and County Bank), in place of its old premises on the corner of the Market Place and Bridge Street Brow. A sculpture above the entrance includes the date 1836, the year in which the Bank of Stockport was established (6.34).[61]

The Covered Market Enclosed

In the latter years of the nineteenth century and early years of the twentieth the open lower sides of the Covered Market were filled in. This effectively turned 'the glass umbrella' into an

Above: 6.27 The Covered Market, showing the first bay to be enclosed

enclosed market hall but it was a piecemeal process. Its beginning has traditionally been associated with Ephraim Marks in the 1890s but as early as 1884 the council had the end bay facing the Manchester and County Bank filled in with timber on a brick foundation (6.27).[62] In 1895-6 Ephraim Marks obtained permission for his stall at the east end of the Covered Market to be enlarged and closed in.[63] Ephraim was the older brother of Michael Marks, the founder of Marks and Spencer Ltd, and after settling in Manchester in 1891 emulated his brother by establishing his own chain of Penny Bazaars.[64] Early in 1898 a second market trader was also allowed to enclose his stall. Other requests soon followed but the council deferred a decision while it awaited the borough surveyor's report on a scheme to construct enclosed stalls all along the north side of the building. A delay followed and for a while the impetus was lost. By 1905, however, the council had started work on enclosing the sides and this process continued, a few stalls at a time, until its completion in 1910.[65]

A number of the stalls in the Covered Market at the beginning of the twenty-first century displayed features which suggest that they dated back to the 1900s. Most of these stalls were located along the northern and southern sides of the building (6.28). Their details included moulded cornices above the stall; wooden counters with a moulded front, above tongue and grove panelling and a skirting with a cast-iron ventilation grill; and, in two cases, wooden roller shuttering with the name plate of the manufacturer G Brady & Co, of Pott Street, Ancoats.[66]

The Covered Market Shortened

In November 1912 the western end of the Covered Market was removed, reducing the building to its present length. The alteration arose from the council's decision to introduce a trolley bus

Above: 6.28 Early market stalls (right)

123

service between Stockport and Offerton. This was one of the earliest such services in the country, and ran from 1913 to 1919 when the trolley buses on the route were replaced by the Corporation's first motor buses. Its proposed route ran via the Market Place, but the Covered Market meant that there was insufficient room. One suggestion was to round off the building's north-west corner but the final decision was for the removal of the entire westernmost bay.[67] The new western wall of the building reused the original exterior columns, but this end of the Covered Market lost the gables and upper tracery which are features of the other end and sides (6.29).

Above: 6.29 The Covered Market enclosed and shortened

WOMBWELL'S
NATIONAL MENAGERIE,
MARKET PLACE, STOCKPORT.

GEORGE WOMBWELL, proprietor of the most magnificent collection of ANIMATED NATURE that ever was exhibited in the British Empire, respectfully announces to the gentry and inhabitants of Stockport and its environs, that his UNEQUALLED COLLECTION OF ZOOLOGY will be open for their inspection during the ensuing May Fair.

In the great moving Castle are THREE ROYAL ELEPHANTS. The large Elephant is acknowledged to be the most stupendous quadruped of the kind ever exhibited in Great Britain. That extraordinary production of nature the great ONE-HORNED RHINOCEROS, or Scripture Unicorn, the finest specimen of the kind now in Europe. Noble Groups of LIONS. The BRITISH LIONESS. Most Beautiful ZEBRAS. A pair of those singular and beautiful animals the GIRAFFES, or CAMELEOPARD. The finest pair of Bengal TIGERS ever imported. Groups of Senegal and Asiatic LEOPARDS; also, that rare animal the BLACK ORIENTAL LEOPARD, the only one in the kingdom. The great POLAR MONSTER from the ARCTIC REGIONS. Just added to the Menagerie the GNU, or the Horned Horse of Africa. Striped and Spotted HYÆNAS, WOLVES, JACKALLS, &c. A pair of those rare animals the MUSTULLA GUBA, or Honey Bears of Africa. Just added to the Menagerie, a very fine specimen of the NYL-GHAU.

The AVIARY contains BIRDS of the most beautiful plumage. The Menagerie also contains the greatest variety of the Semia Genus ever seen.

☞ For particulars see Hand Bills.

Above: 6.30 Advertising the arrival of George Wombwell's Menagerie, 1843

The Fairs

By the mid nineteenth century the number of fairs was on the increase. In the first half of the nineteenth-century there were four, the two fairs in March, the great May fair, and the October fair originally established under the charter of 1260. In 1856 two others were added, in January and July, and in 1885 five more were established, held on the first Friday of February, June, August, September and December. A cattle fair was held on all these occasions, situated from 1879 onwards on the fairground at Portwood.[68]

In the early nineteenth century the May fair was already a great festive occasion during which stalls and fairground attractions were first set up on and around the Market Place and later spilled over to glebe land at Waterloo Road. In the early 1840s the manorial authorities complained to the rector, Charles Kenrick

Prescot, that the presence of a fair at Waterloo Road was an infringement of Lord Vernon's rights. For his part, Prescot disclaimed any responsibility for 'the intrusion of these people' and requested that the steward Thomas Ashworth should 'keep them, their rubbish and their rabble within the limits of the Market Place, and far away from my end of the town'.[69] In 1843 the fair does seem to have been confined to the Market Place and its immediate vicinity, but it was held at a time when the town was beginning to recover from its economic depression and was particularly well attended. On the evening of the first day, 2000 people are said to have left Stockport by the last train, and the fairground attractions continued to draw the crowds for the rest of the week.[70] Among these was George Wombwell's Travelling Menagerie, a collection of exotic animals famous throughout the country (6.30). The menagerie made regular visits to Stockport at the time of the May fair and, after the demolition of Castle Mill in 1841, was set up on Castle Yard.[71]

Above: 6.31 The May fair in Mersey Square, about 1900

Following the congestion of 1843, the use of the Waterloo Road site was resumed. By 1852 it seems to have become the main focal point of the fair, with stalls extending from here to the Market Place. The May fair of 1851 was the first to be held under council administration and seems to have been warmly anticipated by the showmen who attended, 'considerable reduction having been made in the manorial tollage claimed, and some improvement taken place in the men who demanded it, as well as the manner of receiving it'. The previous week no fewer than six travelling attractions were announced on the front page of the *Stockport Advertiser*, comprising Pickul's Splendid Portable Theatre, Messrs Correli and Snape's Roman Amphitheatre, Hylton's Royal Menagerie, Brierley's Circus Royal and Madame Hart's Temple of Magic, as well as Wombwell's own Royal Menagerie. The takings, however, did not live up to expectations and the May fair of the following year was noted for the absence of wild beasts.[72]

The Waterloo fairground continued in use until 1899 when the rector terminated a lease of the site to the Corporation, and a replacement location was then found at Mersey Square in the town centre (6.31).[73] By that period a new overspill site for the May fair had also been found by the Armoury on the west side of the town (6.32).[74] The Portwood fairground remained in use until 1936.[75]

Above: 6.32 The May fair at the Armoury Ground, 1907

Buildings of the Market Place

In the Victorian era, as earlier in the nineteenth century, the shops of the Market Place tended to cater for the better off customer (see Appendix). The north side continued to be characterized by a proliferation of drapers and grocers, joined in the 1840s by the boot and shoe maker George Wild who moved to No 30 Market Place from perhaps less fashionable premises on the south side. One of Stockport's leading hatting firms in the late nineteenth century began from a small-scale operation at No 5 Market Place. Sarah Ward ran a hat-finishing workshop and warehouse here from about 1850, initially along with a confectionary business. The family business expanded into premises on Lower Hillgate and in 1895 moved into Wellington Mill, now the Hat Museum.[76]

Above: 6.33 The Baker's Vaults, built in 1861

The council's improvements to the Market Place in the 1860s prompted a series of other new building works. We have already seen that the Baker's Vaults was erected in 1861 (6.33), the same year as the Covered Market, and that the extension of St Petersgate over the new bridge was followed by the construction in 1868 of the Stockport Bank building, one of the grandest on the Market Place (6.26, 6.34). Next door to the bank, the old Bull's Head is believed to have been rebuilt in about 1867.[77]

Above: 6.34 The entrance to the former Bank of Stockport, built in 1868

George Wild, whose premises at No 30 were part of Staircase House, responded to the building of the new Covered Market by adding a new brick facade to this property. His family name can still be seen in floor tiling in the doorway (6.35).[78]

Other later alterations transformed the west side of the Market Place by creating a row of buildings with a distinctive range of styles and materials. In about 1890 the Angel Inn and adjacent premises were faced with stucco, decorated with motifs which included angels' heads (6.36, 6.37). At about the same time, the neighbouring property of Rostrons the drapers was rebuilt with a facade of red brick and moulded terracotta, in sharp contrast to the older classical style of the adjoining Produce Hall. The architectural mix was completed in the early twentieth century when the premises at the St Petersgate end of this row were rebuilt with a mock-Tudor facade. It recalls the 'Black and White Revival' buildings which between the 1850s and the Edwardian period transformed the centre of Chester.[79] Closer to home, the building also has echoes of the nearby Underbank Hall and was clearly inspired by Stockport's own past.

Above: 6.35 The entrance to Wild's shoe shop, No 30 Market Place

Right: 6.36 The Angel Inn, Samuel Chadwick, tea and coffee dealer, and Rostrons, drapers, about 1880

Below: 6.37 Buildings on the west side of the Market Place, including the former Angel Inn and Rostrons, today

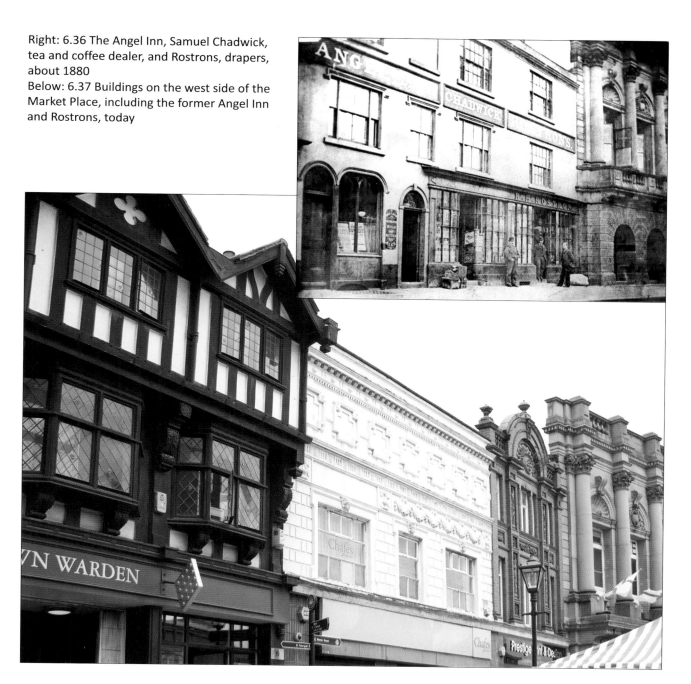

Above: 7.1 Inside the Produce Hall

7. Continuation and Renovation

In March 1945, towards the close of the Second World War, the borough surveyor published a grand design for the future shape of the town. Among the proposals was one to move the market to a more spacious site at Bridgefields, on the north side of the town centre, where there would be a new open-air market and market hall. The Covered Market and other properties on the Market Place would have been demolished and the area given over to car parking and new development.[1] Implementation of the town plan was impractical in the years of post-war austerity, and the market remained on its historic site. Between the 1960s and 1980s, however, successive new schemes were proposed for the redevelopment of that site, involving the construction of a new market hall and the demolition of many of the Market Place's historic buildings. The failure of these plans to come to fruition owed much to the strength of local opposition.

By the 1980s a number of the Market Place's historic buildings were in a state of neglect but there was also now a growing recognition of the value of conservation and repair. The Covered Market was reprieved from demolition and underwent a programme of remedial works. Proposals to demolish Staircase House were successively opposed by a local group, Stockport Heritage Trust.

In the mid 1990s the Market Place and neighbouring streets entered a phase of intensive renovation which continued into the following decade. New buildings were erected on vacant sites to recreate a continuous street frontage (7.3). A few buildings, unsuitable for adaptation, were replaced, although where possible the historic facade was retained. A number of the more important buildings, in a poor state of repair, underwent major restoration. A guiding principle of the overall scheme was to create a complementary mix of uses, including housing, retail and

Above: 7.2 Traditional woodworking techniques were used in the restoration of Staircase House

visitor facilities. At the present time (2010) St Mary's Church is also undergoing a programme of repair and restoration.

Restoration and refurbishment of Staircase House meant that one of the town's most important historic buildings was now open to the public (7.2). The building had suffered particularly badly from years of neglect and a fire in 1995 had destroyed much of the iconic staircase, which was painstakingly remade (7.5).
The interior was recreated as a series of period rooms ranging from the seventeenth century to the home front of the Second World War. Adjoining properties on the Market Place now house the Stockport Story Museum, chronicling the development of the area from prehistoric times to the present day. At No 28 Market Place, the ground floor opened as Blackshaw's Cafe, with a shop front and signage from Blackshaw's Bakery on Hillgate, transferred here from museum storage where these had been preserved since the demolition of the original building in the 1970s. The side wall of No 28 retains a painted advertisement for Emersons, clothes dealers who occupied the premises in the early twentieth century (7.6).

The two great buildings erected by the nineteenth-century borough council to house the market were also

Above: 7.3 The building on the corner of Market Place and Millgate was erected in 1997
Below: 7.4 Detail of the Blue Plaque

given a new lease of life. At the Produce Hall, the floor inserted in the 1870s for the town's library was partly removed and the interior was opened once more to the roof (7.1). The Covered Market underwent a major restoration, undertaken in two phases to allow works to be carried out in one half of the building while trading continued in the other.

In recent years, in an echo of the market's earlier history, trading days have been extended to suit the changing habits of visitors to the market. The Market Place is now host to specialist markets, as well as cultural, leisure and arts activities. The sensitive refurbishment of the area's many fine buildings which survive from key periods of its history has acted as a catalyst for regeneration and is breathing new life into this historic centre, where the only ancient market within Greater Manchester still operating on its original site has evolved over three quarters of a millennium.

Above: 7.5 The recreated Jacobean staircase at Staircase House
Right: 7.6 The Emersons' painted advertisement was found preserved behind a later advertising hoarding

Notes

1. Introduction

1. For detailed accounts of Stockport's history see Heginbotham 1882 & 1892 and Arrowsmith 1997. The most recent account is by Morris Garratt (2009).
2. Wardle & Bentham 1814, 223.
3. Ormerod 1882, vol 3, 545.
4. Arrowsmith 1997, 107-8. The digging of cellars in the sandstone bedrock is documented by the late seventeenth century (CRO DVE 2401/8/3 Deeds relating to a new wall at Castle Hill).
5. Arrowsmith 1997, 11-12.
6. Arrowsmith 1997, 14-16.
7. Some of the supposed 'Roman' finds from Stockport are of dubious authenticity; see Tindall 1985, 69 and Arrowsmith 1997, 18-19.

2. The Medieval Market Place

1. For the general development of Stockport in this period see Arrowsmith 1997, 29-64. The authoritative account on the meaning of Stockport's place-name is Dodgson 1970, 294-5.
2. Arrowsmith 1997, 40-1; Laughton 2008, 7.
3. On Geoffrey de Costentin and Stockport's castle see also Arrowsmith 1997, 31-4.
4. William Stukeley's description of Stockport in 1725 (published posthumously in 1776) refers to 'a place called the Castle Yard walled in' (Heginbotham 1892, 96).
5. Watson 1782, vol 2, 190.
6. Dent 1977.
7. Arrowsmith 1997, 43. Heginbotham 1892, 90, however, believed the 'maner place' to be a building later known as Old Farm on Newbridge Lane.
8. CRO DVE 2401 Stockport box 2, bundle 51, Agreement about stalls in the Castle Yard, 1775.

9. CRO DVE 2401/8/3 Deeds relating to a new wall at Castle Hill.
10. Watkin 1886, 294.

11. Arrowsmith *et al* 2004.
12. Kay 1896; Dent 1977.
13. Arrowsmith 1996, 28-31; SLHL Hurst Scrapbooks vol 4, 99: 'It is fairly certain this gargoyle came from Stockport parish church, demolished in 1810'.
14. 'The Bastile Room or place, containing 20 yards in length and 10 in breadth' was one of two parcels 'in the Market Sted' which Edward Warren granted to William Nicholson in 1537, the other 'lying upon the Castle Hill on the east and north' (Earwaker 1877, 350). In 1639 Francis Nicholson sold back to a later Edward Warren several burgages and shops in the Market Place, known as the 'Bastile houses' (CRO DVE 2401/1/1, f 37).
15. Watson's transcription survives in his manuscript collection towards a history of Cheshire in the Bodleian Library (MS. Top. Cheshire b.1. f 204), and was copied and translated by Heginbotham (1892, 297).
16. Morris 1983, 25.
17. Stewart-Brown 1925, 209; Highet 1960, 54, 73; Stewart-Brown 1916, 47.
18. CRO DVE 9/39; SLHL Proclamations for the fair, 1842, 1844, 1846.
19. Heginbotham 1892, 262-3. The inauguration of the mayor during St Wilfrid's fair is documented from at least 1703 (SLHL Diary of William Davenport, 1700-5).
20. Arrowsmith 1997, 37.
21. Stewart-Brown 1925, 215, 230.
22. The charter is transcribed and translated by Heginbotham 1892, 291-3.
23. Tait 1904, 46-7, 111-14, 199, 202.
24. Davies 1961, 7-9 (Macclesfield); Tait 1904 (Lancashire); Laughton 2008, 6, 8 Table 1.1 (Cheshire).
25. Arrowsmith 1997, 40.
26. Tindall 1985, 71; Arrowsmith 1997, 42-4, 56; Blome 1673, 57.
27. Burke & Arrowsmith 1995; Nevell *et al* 2004.
28. Arrowsmith 2004.
29. Nevell *et al* 2004, 15; Arrowsmith 1996, 17-18.
30. Dent 1977, 7-8. Exploratory excavations on a neighbouring area in 1984 revealed post-holes, gullies and a cobbled area; this site also produced a small quantity of medieval pottery (Tindall 1985, 72).
31. Nevell *et al* 2004.
32. Arrowsmith 1997, 41 & 2004, 43. In the sixteenth century William Dodge's house on the Market Place was owned by the Elcock family, on whom see pp 47-8.
33. Arrowsmith 1997, 59-61.
34. Heginbotham 1882, 186-207; Richards 1947, 309-10; Arrowsmith 1997, 62; Architectural History Practice/ Stockport Council 2005.

3. 'A populous and great markett towne', 1500-1700

1. For more detailed accounts of the town in this period see Arrowsmith 1997, 65-96, and Phillips 1998.
2. The map, coded E:l:r 257, was among the papers of the Warren family in 1730 (CRO DVE 2401/1/1, f 52).
3. Taylor 1974, Appendix V.
4. CRO DVE 2401/15 Stockport Easter book 1619.
5. Ormerod 1882, vol 3, 545-6; Taylor 1974, 33-4.
6. Taylor 1974, Appendix II. In 1707 there was a dispute between Stockport and Congleton regarding the tolls of Stockport (CRO DVE 2401/1/1, f 102).
7. Blome 1673, 57.
8. CRO DVE 2401/1/1, f 48; Bodleian Library MS. Top. Cheshire b.1. ff 204-5.
9. CRO DDX 23/2 Diary of a Cheshire Farmer, Mr John Ryle, 1649-1721. This is a later copy of the original document and was in turn transcribed by Frank Mitchell in 1972 (in SLHL).
10. SLHL Stockport Court Leet Records 1661-7; Taylor 1974, 19-24 & Appendix II.
11. SLHL Stockport Court Leet Records 2 Oct 1662.
12. Phillips & Smith 1985, 45-6 & 1992, 252-61; Arrowsmith 1997, 72.
13. Phillips & Smith 1992, 159-65.
14. CRO DDX 69/9; Gibson 1863, 83-92. The records of the Legh family of Lyme Park show that in the 1720s and 1730s they bought corn, groceries, ironmongery, cloth,

shoes and paper at Stockport, but also made purchases in Macclesfield. In the 1730s and 1740s the Ardernes of Arden Hall in Bredbury regularly shopped in Stockport but also bought cloth in Manchester and plate in London (Mitchell 1984, 262).

15. CRO DVE 2401/1/1, f 48; Bodleian Library MS. Top. Cheshire b.1. ff 204-5; Heginbotham 1892, 410.
16. Heginbotham 1892, 109.
17. Nevell 1998. During the renovation and rebuilding works the southern half of the east wall collapsed, but was later reconstructed. At the time of the collapse only a partial survey had been undertaken. No final report has been compiled for this site, which would still repay further study.
18. Heginbotham 1892, 261; CRO DVE 2401/1/1, f 38.
19. Tupling 1945-6, 4-5, 11.
20. CRO DVE 2401/13 Stockport manor rental 1545.
21. Tupling 1945-6, 5-7.
22. Thorp 1940, 156,
23. Judicial hearings were also held in the 'Court House'. In 1630 the court leet ordered that the mayor 'for the time being should not hear or examine any cases of malefactors in any private house or chamber but only in the Court House'. In 1661 the mayor William Beeley heard the case of Thomas Wasse in 'the Comon Hall or Court House' (Heginbotham 1892, 262, 264-5).
24. SLHL Stockport Court Leet Records 14 May 1663.
25. CRO DVE 8/3/6; Heginbotham 1892, 300.
26. CRO DVE 2401/1/1, f 108.
27. Greenhalgh 1887, 243.
28. Heginbotham 1882, 263.
29. Wild (1896, 77) recorded that 'An old painting in the possession of the descendants of Mr Tucker, formerly an official under the Corporation, had an inscription on the back stating that the painting was intended for the Stockport cross'. An engraving made from the painting shows a three-stepped plinth and a square shaft with a ball finial carrying a female classical figure with raised arms. The original painting is said to show the cross in a rustic setting.
30. Wild 1896.
31. Heginbotham 1892, 98-9; Arrowsmith 2004, 29.
32. Defoe 1778, 343-4; Aikin 1795, 445. In 1758 Sir George Warren, the lord of the manor, was granted the right to the water in the Barn Fields by the landowner William Wright (CRO DVE 2401/1/1, f 108).
33. Arrowsmith 1997, 195.
34. Nevell *et al* 2004, 16-18; Greater Manchester Historic Environment Record 14795, held by the Greater Manchester Archaeological Unit.
35. Arrowsmith 1997, 72.
36. Heginbotham 1882, 123-4.
37. Heginbotham 1882, 171 & 1892, 261-2.
38. Heginbotham 1892, 264-5; Taylor 1974, Appendix V; Phillips 1998, 42.
39. Taylor 1974, 28; Heginbotham 1882, 173.
40. Heginbotham 171, 173-5; Burton Mss vol 9, 185, 189; Thorp 1940, 157-8, 197.
41. Taylor 1974, 29; Heginbotham 1882, 171-3.
42. Arrowsmith 1996, 32-3.
43. There is a succession of reports on Staircase House but as yet no single definitive account. The preliminary work by W J Smith (1977) was followed by more detailed studies by the Greater Manchester Archaeological Unit (Hartwell & Bryant 1985), the Royal Commission for the Historical Monuments of England (RCHME 1993), and most fully by Greater Manchester Archaeological Contracts in 1994, reported in Burke & Arrowsmith 1995 and summarized in Arrowsmith 1996, 15-27. This last study is supplemented by Nevell *et al* 2004, which includes the results of survey work and archaeological recording carried out from 1999 onwards during the restoration of the building. Some features uncovered during that restoration, including the kitchen chimney in the stone wing and the western elevation of the rear wing, remain unreported.
44. Arrowsmith 2004, 42-4.
45. Arrowsmith 2004, 25-37.
46. SLHL Hurst Scrapbooks vol 5, 131-2: Godfrey 1911, 35 Fig 28, 48-54.

47. CRO DVE 2401/15 Stockport Easter book 1619. The other streets listed are Churchgate (27 households), Millgate (49), Underbank (70), and Hillgate (120). On the Easter book see Phillips 1998, 45-7.
48. Arrowsmith 2004, 39-40.
49. Phillips & Smith 1992, 166-7, 243-8.
50. Heginbotham 1882, 100-1, 282.
51. CRO DVE 2401/1/11.

4. The Market Place of the Silk Town, 1700-80

1. For the general development of Stockport in this period see Arrowsmith 1997, 97-124.
2. Defoe 1769, 397.
3. SLHL HX 182.
4. Aikin 1795, 45, 446; Greenhalgh 1887, 18.
5. Defoe 1769, 397.
6. Aikin 1795, 203; Mitchell 1975, 133.
7. Thorp 1940, 160-1, 165.
8. Thorp 1940, 160.
9. Thorp 1940, 164-6.
10. Defoe 1769, 397; CRO DVE 2401/1/1, f 48.
11. For the life of Sir George Warren see Giles 1990. A summary of his disputes over the manor is given by Arrowsmith 1997, 118-19.
12. SLHL HX 229 (partly published in Taylor 1974, 35-6).
13. SLHL HX 182.
14. Thorp 1940, 159, 168; Heginbotham 1892, 120; CRO DVE 2401/20 Stockport rentals 1785, 1786-7.
15. The lower estimate is from J H Hanshall in 1823, cited by Porter 1976, 141, and higher figure from Henry Holland in 1808, cited by Foster 1998, 24. In 1729 a total of 5776 tons of 'Cheshire cheese' was shipped to London, but the term also included cheeses made in neighbouring counties; a modern estimate places the annual production of 'Cheshire cheese' at that date perhaps at about 15,000 tons, with about half of this made in Cheshire itself (Foster 1998, 8).
16. Gregory et al 2008.
17. CRO DVE 2401/2/12 (partial copy in SLHL Hurst Scrapbooks vol 1, 117-21).
18. CRO DVE 3282; Giles 1950-1, 79-80.
19. In the 1880s John Greenhalgh recalled the mill as being two storeys high but this does not appear to be borne out by the contemporary illustrations (Greenhalgh 1888, 64).
20. CRO DVE 2401 Stockport Box 2, bundle 51, Agreement about stalls in the Castle Yard, 1775. Lysons & Lysons 1810, 778 may also refer to this original scheme, describing Castle Mill as 'a large circular building on the site of the castle, built by the late Sir George Warren, the lord of the manor, for a market-house'.
21. Giles 1950, 56-7 & 1950-1, 80-2.
22. Glen 1984, 67-8.
23. Watson 1782, vol 2, 190; Andrews 1935, 179.
24. CRO DVE 2401/2/12 Counterpart lease of the Castle Yard, 1778.
25. Glen 1979; Giles 1950, 55-6.
26. Burton Mss vol 5, 533.
27. Lysons & Lysons 1810, 778. On the rise and fall of muslin manufacture in Stockport see Arrowsmith 1997, 134-6.
28. Radcliffe 1828, 12-14.
29. Arrowsmith et al 2004.
30. Andrews 1935, 179.
31. Smith 1977, 20.
32. Heginbotham 1882, 69. For the 'Forty-five' in Stockport see Arrowsmith 1997, 119-21.
33. SLHL Stockport Poor Rate Book 1731.
34. Heginbotham 1892, 318.
35. The bricks and tiles were originally believed to be Roman or medieval (Middleton 1899, 6; Cheshire Notes and Queries 1896, 83, 143 & 1902, 153). Material from the site is held in Stockport's reserve collection. Bricks and a perforated tile were donated by the Stockport Museum Committee to Warrington Museum in 1898, and according to a display label were 'found at a depth of 6 feet, Market Place, Stockport' (Craig Sherwood, Warrington Central Library, Museum and Art Gallery, personal communication). I am grateful to Peter Crew

for comments on the perforated tile, which is of the IC type; see Crew 2004.

5. The Market Place of the Cotton Town, 1780-1840

1. On the economic and social development of Stockport at this period see Giles 1950, and Arrowsmith 1997, 125-214.
2. *Bradshaw's Journal* 16 July 1842, quoted by Ashmore 1975, 65.
3. On William Shuttleworth (1785-1829) see Heginbotham 1892, 353-4.
4. Aikin 1795, 446; Lysons & Lysons 1810, 777; Butterworth 1827, 246; Giles 1950, 459.
5. Mitchell 1984, 273-5; Giles 1950, 502-3; PP 1842 XXXV, 99. The number of hawkers was probably also on the increase in the early nineteenth century (Mitchell 1984, 269-70).
6. Mitchell 1982, 45-7 & 1984, 264-5.
7. CRO DVE 9/27; PP 1847 XIX, 12.
8. The 1822 and 1838 lists are included in CRO DVE 2401/1/1; the circa 1802 list is copied in Burton Mss vol 9, 43-4.
9. SLHL B/KK/23/18; CRO DVE 9/27. In June 1843 the solicitor Hudson claimed that until recently the tolls demanded were much lower than the printed list (SA 2 June 1843), but Stride's testimony shows this to be unreliable.
10. Aikin 1795, 443; Giles 1950, 454 & 1950-1, 84-5.
11. Greenhalgh 1887, 243.
12. Thorp 1940, 149-50; Giles 1950, 109-10.
13. Burton Mss vol 5, 473.
14. Thorp 1940, 146.
15. Heginbotham 1882, 175.
16. CRO DVE 9/26.
17. CRO P14/3435/6/2; Heginbotham 1882, 246.
18. Heginbotham 1892, 100. The row is shown on the 1770 map and presumably included at least some of the '13 small shops adjoining the church yard' at that date (CRO DVE 3282).
19. SA 18 Mar 1825.
20. CRO DVE 9/26.
21. Gregory *et al* 2008.
22. Loverseed 1997, 5.
23. SA 6 February 1824; Giles 1950, 455-6.
24. Greenhalgh 1887, 253; SA 28 July 1823.
25. Giles 1950, 330 n 1.
26. Giles 1950, 456; SA 6 February 1824, 13 September 1843.
27. In about 1834 the butchers' booths were transferred from the south to the north side of the Market Place (CRO DVE 9/27).
28. SA 9 July 1824; Butterworth 1827, 274.
29. SA 25 Dec 1829; Lewis 1831, 183; SLHL Hurst Scrapbooks vol 8, 192.
30. CRO DVE 9/29 describes the New Market as 'set up by Mr Winterbottom'. His stewardship is recorded in SLHL Stockport Court Leet Book 1799-1833 & 1834-58.
31. SLHL Stockport Court Leet Book 1834-58.
32. SLHL Stockport Court Leet Book 1834-58, copy of letters re market in Hillgate 23 & 26 July 1842; CRO DVE 9/29.
33. SA 19 1844.
34. SLHL Hurst Scrapbooks vol 8, 192.
35. Lysons & Lysons 1810, 778; Lewis 1831, 183. Holland (1808, 313-14) includes Stockport among the Cheshire fairs which were 'principally for the sale of cows, horses, pigs, cloth, linen, hardware and pedlary goods'.
36. Heginbotham 1892, 262; Greenhalgh 1886, 111.
37. SA Supplement 22 May & 5 June 1885, 'Old Stockport' XCVI & XCVII.
38. Heginbotham 1892, 118; CRO DVE 9/25.
39. CRO DVE 9/27; SA 5 May 1843; PP 1847 XIX, 3.
40. Robinson 1977, 9; SA 15 & 22 June, 6 & 13 July 1827. A third and less successful ascent, by Mr Graham, was made the following year (SA 7 &14 November 1828; Loverseed 1997, 6).
41. Butterworth 1827, 247.
42. According to John Greenhalgh, the Rose and Crown, at No 3 Market Place, stayed open all day and night for the benefit of people travelling to the market from a

distance, although this also meant the place developed a reputation as a drinking den. In the 1820s the pub was also the departure point for a local carrier, John Turner, who twice a week conveyed goods between Stockport and Ashton (Greenhalgh 1888, 32; Baines 1825, 730). The Rose and Crown closed in 1846-7. The Sun closed in 1936 and the Angel in 1951. The Pack Horse was in existence in 1795; this was a timber-framed building which was demolished in 1931 and replaced by the present mock-Tudor building (Horrocks nd).

43. Mitchell 1984, 275-7.
44. Giles 1950, 504.
45. Arrowsmith 2004, 21-4.
46. Burke & Arrowsmith 1995, 11.
47. Burke & Arrowsmith 1995, 11 & Table 1.
48. Arrowsmith 2004, 38.
49. Andrews 1935, 179; Aikin 1795, 443; Heginbotham 1882, 188, 211.
50. Architectural History Practice/Stockport Council 2005; Heginbotham 1882, 210-23; Giles 1950, 529-33; Robinson 1979, 150. Drawings by Wyatt for St Mary's are held at Sir John Soane's Museum, London.
51. Heginbotham 1882, 193, 223, 323-4; Architectural History Practice/Stockport Council 2005.
52. Heginbotham 1882, 70-1; SLHL Hurst Scrapbooks vol 8, 61-2.
53. Mitchell 1982, 63. In 1788 Norbury had been fined £50, after being found guilty of mixing good wheat with putrid pastry and wheat infected with grubs, grinding this up and selling it as flour. His dealings in corn made him a wealthy man and the owner of property in both Stockport and Marple. When he died in 1813 his personal estate was valued at £17,500 (Mitchell 1975, 326, 335-6). His tomb at Marple occupies a prime position to the east of the old All Saints' Church.
54. Mitchell 1975, 188 & 1982, 57.
55. Glen 1984, 124.
56. For a summary of the events of 1816-19 see Arrowsmith 1997, 198-202. The fullest account is by Glen (1984).

57. Heginbotham 1882, 79-81; Giles 1950, 176-8; Glen 1984, 206-7.
58. Burton Mss vol 5, 775.
59. Reid 1974, 108-14, 242. After the arrest of Stephens in December 1838, the venue shifted to the Stanley Arms on Newbridge Lane.

6. An Age of Improvements, 1840-1912

1. For more details on the development of Stockport from 1840 to the early twentieth century see Arrowsmith 1997, 215-52.
2. Taylor 1974, 40; SLHL Stockport Court Leet Book 1834-58.
3. PP 1847 XIX, 12.
4. *Advertiser Notes and Queries* I, 1882, 202-3, reprinted from *Stockport Monthly Magazine* December 1840. In 1847 it was reported that traders from Wilmslow were using the railway to sell goods in Manchester rather than at Stockport, while the opening of railway link in 1845 between Manchester and the Ashton-under-Lyne and Mottram-in-Longdendale area is also said to have drawn people away from Stockport (PP 1847 XIX, 9, 17).
5. SA 19 August 1842; PP 1842 XXXV, 99-100; SA 9 June 1843.
6. Heginbotham 1882, 13; Greenhalgh 1888, 64.
7. CRO DVE 9/26.
8. CRO D 6732 List of tolls on fair and market days, 1842; SA 2 June 1843.
9. In 1843 Castle Yard was described as being 'reserved as a stand for cattle' (SA 6 Oct 1843).
10. SA 13 May & 3 June 1842; CRO DVE 9/26.
11. SA 29 July 1842, 21 April 1843.
12. SA13 May 1842; CRO DVE 9/4.
13. SA 16 & 23 May, 19 September 1851.
14. PP 1847 XIX, 10-11.
15. SA 2 June 1843.
16. SA 9 June 1843; SLHL B/KK/23/18; SA 17 November 1843.
17. PP 1847 XIX, 12, 14.
18. SA 1 September 1843.

19. SA 21 April 1843.
20. SLHL B/KK/23/18; SA 8 & 15 September, 17 November 1843.
21. SA 20 December 1844, 24 January 1845.
22. Arrowsmith 2006, 9-10.
23. SA 20 December 1844, 24 January 1845.
24. SA 25 April & 16 May 1845.
25. SA 19 September 1851.
26. 10 & 11 Vic. Ch. cclxxxiv (1847); Heginbotham 1892, 275.
27. PP 1847 XIX; Smith 1938, 407; Taylor 1974, 42-4.
28. Heginbotham 1892, 275; SA 28 June 1850.
29. SLHL Court Leet Book 1834-58; Taylor 1974, 45 & Appendix IV.
30. SA 28 June & 19 July 1850; Greenhalgh 1888, 65.
31. SA 20 June, 12 & 19 September 1851, 14 May 1852; *The Builder* X no 476, 20 March 1852, 184; Schmiechen & Carls 1999, 292.
32. Chaplin nd, no 30.
33. SA 16 & 23 May 1851.
34. SA 14 February 1851; SLHL Typescript notes of MMTC 10 & 24 November 1852, 5 January 1853.
35. Bagshaw 1850, 176; SA 6 May 1853; SLHL Typescript notes of MMTC 22 December 1852, 1 February, 13 April & 10 November 1853. The date at which the cattle market was moved from Castle Yard to Mersey Street has not been identified.
36. Astle 1922, 36.
37. Arrowsmith *et al* 2004, 14-16, 25.
38. Heginbotham 1892, 279.
39. SLHL MMTC 1896-1902, Notice for fairs and markets for horses, cattle, sheep and pigs, April 1893; 6 & 20 February 1900 (sale of pigs in Castle Yard). On Saturday Castle Yard formed part of the general market for provisions (SLHL MMTC 13 July 1897).
40. SLHL MMTC 18 December 1894.
41. SLHL MMTC 16 July 1895.
42. Smith 1994, 10; SLHL Typescript notes of MMTC 19 July, 24 October, 8 November 1854.
43. Greenhalgh 1888, 64-5.
44. Heginbotham 1892, 279-80; SA 10 May 1878, 12 March 1880. The architect was T H Allen.
45. SA 3 February & 30 March 1860.
46. SLHL MMTC 2 & 30 May, 9, 11 & 25 July, 8 & 22 August, 4 September 1860; SA 13, 20 & 27 April, 8 June, 17 August 1860.
47. SA 7 September 1860; *The Builder* XVIII no 919, 15 September 1860, 591.
48. *The Builder* XI no 553, 10 September 1853, 578; SA 17 May 1861; Schmiechen & Carls 1999, 118, 298 (Wolverhampton), 262 (Derby).
49. SLHL MMTC 15 February 1861.
50. SLHL MMTC 23 November & 7 December 1864, 4 January, 7 June & 2 August 1865.
51. SA 6 August 1875.
52. SA 17 May 1860.
53. SLHL MMTC 17 April, 28 August & 4 September 1861.
54. SLHL MMTC 16 May 1861.
55. SLHL MMTC 24 October 1861; SA 17 June 1862.
56. SLHL MMTC 29 May, 4 & 12 June 1861.
57. Schmiechen & Carls 1999, 176-7.
58. SA 6 Oct 1865; Heginbotham 1892, 277.
59. Heginbotham 1892, 415.
60. Heginbotham 1892, 277; Galvin 1986, no 105; Astle 1922, 123.
61. SA 21 February 1868; Heginbotham 1892, 426.
62. SLHL MMTC 29 January, 12 February 1884.
63. SLHL MMTC 17 December 1895, 14 January & 25 February 1896.
64. Information kindly provided by The Marks & Spencer Company Archive. There is no known evidence that Ephraim ever ran any M&S Penny Bazaars but, following the death of Michael Marks, he was a shareholder in the company.
65. SLHL MMTC 6 January, 22 March, 5 April & 29 November 1898. The minutes contain numerous references to the building of new stalls on the sides of the Covered Market between 14 November 1905 and 31 May 1910; see Arrowsmith *et al* 2005, 23-5.
66. Arrowsmith *et al* 2005, 27.

67. SLHL MMTC 20 August & 6 September 1912;
    Stockport County Borough 1960.
68. Heginbotham 1892, 281, 410; SLHL MMTC 1896-1902,
    Notice for fairs and markets for horses, cattle, sheep
    and pigs, April 1893.
69. CRO DVE 9/25 & 9/28.
70. SA 5 May 1843.
71. Greenhalgh 1888, 242.
72. SA 2 & 9 May 1851, 14 May 1852.
73. SLHL MMTC 10 March 1885, 14 March & 16 May 1899,
    17 April 1900, 3 March 1901; SA 8 May 1900.
74. SLHL MMTC 5 & 19 April 1887.
75. County Borough of Stockport 1960.
76. McKnight 2000, 62. Survey work carried out by the
    University of Manchester Archaeological Unit ahead of
    rebuilding at No 5 Market Place found that the roof
    space had been modified in the mid to late nineteenth
    century to create a large workshop or warehouse.
77. Horrocks nd; Architectural History Practice/Stockport
    Council 2005.
78. Astle 1922, 122.
79. Carrington 1994, 109-11.

7. Continuation and Renovation

1. Stockport County Borough 1945; Stockport Express
   1946, 11.

Bibliography

Abbreviations

CRO — Cheshire Record Office
MMTC — Minutes of the Manorial Tolls Committee
SA — *Stockport Advertiser*
SLHL — Stockport Local Heritage Library

Primary

Parliamentary Papers and Acts

PP 1842 XXXV Report into the State of the Population of Stockport.
PP 1847 XIX Minutes of Evidence upon a Preliminary Inquiry
  Respecting the Stockport Manorial Tolls and Bridges Bill.
10 & 11 Vic. Ch. cclxxxiv (1847) An Act to purchase and define the
  Manorial and Market Rights of Stockport, to establish
  public Parks, to purchase or lease Waterworks, to build
  Bridges, and to make other Communications within the
  Borough of Stockport (SLHL).

Bodleian Library

MS Top. Cheshire b.1, Watson Manuscripts, Collections for a history of Cheshire (photographic copy in SLHL).

Cheshire Record Office

D 6732 List of tolls on fair and market days, 1842.
DDX 23/2 Diary of a Cheshire Farmer, Mr John Ryle, 1649-1721.
DDX 69/9 Account book of Henry Bradshaw, 1637-44.
DVE 8/3/6 Stockport manor rental, nd.
DVE 9/4 Petition re Market House, 1844 (copy in SLHL Stockport Court Leet Book 1834-58).
DVE 9/25 Letter re May fair, 3 May 1841.
DVE 9/26 Case and Opinion of Mr Starkie, 1842 (copy in SLHL Stockport Court Leet Book 1834-58).
DVE 9/27 Statement of William Stride, 1843 (copy in SLHL Stockport Court Leet Book 1834-58).
DVE 9/28 Letter re fairs, January 25 1843.
DVE 9/29 Letter re Hillgate market, 25 January 1843.
DVE 9/39 Proclamations for Stockport fair, 1845, 1847.
DVE 2401 Stockport box 2, bundle 51, Agreement about stalls in the Castle Yard, 1775.
DVE 2401/1/1 An Account of Mr Warren's Deeds taken Christmas 1730.
DVE 2401/1/11 Papers re watercourse in Stockport, nd.
DVE 2401/2/12 Counterpart lease of the Castle Yard, 1778.

DVE 2401/8/3 Deeds relating to a new wall at Castle Hill, 1685.

DVE 2401/13 Stockport manor rentals.

DVE 2401/15 Stockport Easter book 1619-29.

DVE 2401/20 (part) Stockport rentals 1785, 1786-7.

DVE 3282 A survey with Maps of the Manor of Poynton the Town of Stockport and sundry Farms & Tenements in the County of Chester belonging to the Hon. Sir George Warren K.B., 1770.

P 14/3435/5/4&5 Plans of pews contained in the nave and aisles, and galleries of the Parish Church of Stockport, 1810.

P 14/3435/6/1 St Mary's Church, Ground Plan of the Church Yard taken when rebuilt in 1817.

P 14/3435/6/2 St Mary's Church, Licence to add part of the churchyard to an adjoining street, 1818.

Stockport Local Heritage Library

Diary of William Davenport, 1700-5.

Minutes of the Manorial Tolls Committee, 1860-1912.

Proclamations for the fair, 1842, 1844, 1846.

Stockport Court Leet Book 1799-1833.

Stockport Court Leet Book 1834-58.

Stockport Court Leet Records 1661-7.

Stockport Poor Rate Book 1731.

B/KK/23/18 Case and opinion of Mr Vaughan Williams, 1843.

HX 182 The case of Sir George Warren touching his rights as lord of the manor, circa 1767.

HX 229 Testimony of Peter Bostock and others relating to the tolls of cheese, 1770.

Secondary

Aikin J 1795 *A Description of the Country from Thirty to Forty Miles Round Manchester*, London (reprinted 1969, New York, Augustus M Kelley).

Andrews C B 1935 *The Torrington Diaries*, vol 2, London, Eyre & Spottiswoode.

Architectural History Practice/Stockport Council 2005 Stockport List Partial Review, unpublished.

Arrowsmith P 1996 *Recording Stockport's Past: Recent Investigations of Historic Sites in the Borough of Stockport*, Stockport Metropolitan Borough Council.

Arrowsmith P 1997 *Stockport: A History*, Stockport Metropolitan Borough Council.

Arrowsmith P 2004 'The Historical Development of Staircase House', in Nevell *et al*, 19-44.

Arrowsmith P 2006 *St Thomas' Hospital, Stockport: Building Development Documentary Research*, unpublished report, University of Manchester Archaeological Unit.

Arrowsmith P, Askew S & Bell S 2004 *Archaeological works at The Courts and Castle Yard, Stockport*, unpublished report, University of Manchester Archaeological Unit.

Arrowsmith P, Nevell M & Hradil I 2005 *Stockport Market Hall: An Archaeological and Historical Assessment of the 1861 Market Hall*, unpublished report, University of Manchester Archaeological Unit.

Ashmore O 1975 *The Industrial Archaeology of Stockport*, University of Manchester Department of Extra Mural Studies.

Astle W (ed) 1922 *"Stockport Advertiser" Centenary History of Stockport*, Stockport, Swain & Co.

Bagshaw S 1850 *History, Gazetteer and Directory of the County of Chester*, Sheffield.

Baines E 1825 *History, Directory, and Gazetteer of the County of Lancaster,* vol 2, Liverpool (reprinted by David & Charles, Newton Abbot).

Blome R 1673 *Britannia: or, a geographical description of the kingdoms of England, Scotland, and Ireland*, London.

Burke T & Arrowsmith P 1995 *Staircase House: Historic Building Survey*, unpublished report, Greater Manchester Archaeological Contracts.

Burton A 1887-9 *A Chronological History of the Town and Neighbourhood of Stockport*, Burton Mss vols 5 & 9 (SLHL microfilm copy of original in Manchester Central Library).

Butterworth J 1827 *A History and Description of the Towns and Parishes of Stockport, Ashton-under-Lyne, Mottram-long-den-dale, and Glossop*, Manchester.

Carrington P 1994 *Chester*, London B T Batsford/English Heritage.

Chaplin J (ed) nd *Stockport History Trail: A stroll through the town's past,* Stockport, Specialised Technical Services.

County Borough of Stockport 1960 *700 Years History of Stockport Market (1260-1960)*.

Crew P 2004 'Perforated Tiles from Corn Driers and Malt Kilns' *British Brick Society Information* 95, 4-12.

Davies C S (ed) 1961 *A History of Macclesfield*, Manchester University Press.

Defoe D & others 1769 *A Tour through the Whole Island of Great Britain*, seventh edition, London.

Defoe D & others 1778 *A Tour through the Whole Island of Great Britain*, eighth edition, London.

Dent J S 1977 'Recent Excavations on the Site of Stockport Castle' *Transactions of the Lancashire and Cheshire Antiquarian Society* 79, 1-13.

Dodgson J McN 1970 *The Place-names of Cheshire, Part I,* English Place-name Society 44 (for 1966-7), Cambridge University Press.

Earwaker J P 1877/80 *East Cheshire Past and Present: A History of the Hundred of Macclesfield, in the County Palatine of Chester from Original Records*, 2 vols, London.

Foster C F 1998 *Cheshire cheese and farming in the North West in the 17th and 18th centuries*, Arley Hall Press.

Galvin F 1986 *Stockport Town Trail*, Stockport Metropolitan Borough Leisure Services Division.

Garratt M 2009 *Stockport: A History*, Chichester, Phillimore & Co.

Gibson A C 1862-3 'Everyday Life of a Country Gentleman of Cheshire in the 17th Century: as shewn in the private expenditure journal of Colonel Henry Bradshaw, of Marple and Wybersleigh' *Transactions of the Historic Society of Lancashire and Cheshire 2*, 67-92.

Giles P M 1950 *The Economic and Social Development of Stockport 1815-36*, unpublished MA thesis, University of Manchester.

Giles P M 1950-1 'The Enclosure of Common Lands in Stockport' *Transactions of the Lancashire and Cheshire Antiquarian Society* 62, 73-110.

Giles P M 1990 'The Last of the Warrens: Sir George Warren, K.B. (1735-1801)' *Transactions of the Historic Society of Lancashire and Cheshire* 140, 47-78.

Glen R 1979 'The Milnes of Stockport and the Export of English Technology during the Early Industrial Revolution' *Cheshire History* 3, 15-21.

Glen R 1984 *Urban Workers in the Industrial Revolution*, Croom Helm.

Godfrey W H 1911 *The English Staircase*, London, Batsford.

Greenhalgh J 1886-9 'Recollections of Stockport', in *Cheshire Notes and Queries* 6-9.

Gregory R, Arrowsmith P, Gregory L & Garratt R 2008 *Stockport Market Place, Phase 1 and 2: An Archaeological Watching Brief and Excavation*, unpublished report, University of Manchester Archaeological Unit.

Hartwell C & Bryant S R 1985 'A Measured Survey of the Buildings at Numbers 30A and 31 Market Place, Stockport', *Greater Manchester Archaeological Journal* 1, 75-88.

Heginbotham H 1882/1892 *Stockport: Ancient and Modern*, 2 vols, London, Sampson Low, Marston & Co.

Highet T P 1960 *The Early History of the Davenports of Davenport*, Chetham Society, 3rd series, 9.

Holland H 1808 *General View of the Agriculture of Cheshire*, London.

Horrocks P nd *A Directory of Public Houses in Stockport*, unpublished manuscript, SLHL.

Hurst J nd Scrapbooks, SLHL.

Kay T 1896 'Remains of the Town Wall of Stockport' *Transactions of the Lancashire and Cheshire Antiquarian Society* 14, 55-61.

Laughton J 2008 *Life in a Late Medieval City: Chester 1275-1520*, Oxford, Windgather Press.

Lewis S 1831 *A Topographical Dictionary of England*, vol 4, London.

Loverseed D 1997 *The Green Giant. The History of the Stockport Gas Undertaking 1820-1949*, privately published.

Lysons Revd D & Lysons S 1810 *Magna Britannia*, vol 2, part 2, London.

McKnight P 2000 *Stockport Hatting*, Stockport MBC Community Services Division.

Middleton T 1899 *Annals of Hyde and District*, Manchester, Cartwright & Rattray.

Minutes of the Manorial Tolls Committee 1852-75, typescript in Folder S/H 58, SLHL.

Mitchell I 1984 'The development of urban retailing, 1700-1815', in P Clark (ed) *The Transformation of English Provincial Towns, 1600-1800*, London, Hutchinson & Co.

Mitchell S I 1975 *Urban Markets and Retail Distribution, 1730-1815, with Particular Reference to Macclesfield, Stockport and Chester*, unpublished DPhil thesis, Oxford University.

Mitchell S I 1980 'Retailing in Eighteenth and Early Nineteenth-century Cheshire' *Transactions of the Historic Society of Lancashire and Cheshire* 130, 36-60.

Mitchell S I 1982 'Food Shortages and Public Order in Cheshire, 1757-1812' *Transactions of the Lancashire and Cheshire Antiquarian Society* 81, 42-66.

Morris M 1983 *Medieval Manchester: A Regional Study, The Archaeology of Greater Manchester*, vol 1, Greater Manchester Archaeological Unit.

Nevell M 1998 *No 1 Mealhouse Brow and Nos 7 & 8 Market Place, Stockport: Interim Building Survey Report*, unpublished report, University of Manchester Archaeological Unit.

Nevell M, Arrowsmith P, McNeil R, Roberts J & Wilson P 2004 *Staircase House, Market Place, Stockport: Archaeological Investigations 1999-2004, Final Report*, unpublished report, University of Manchester Archaeological Unit.

Ormerod G 1882 *The History of the County Palatine and City of Chester*, 3 vols, second edition, revised and enlarged by T Helsby, London, Routledge and Sons.

Phillips C B 1998 'Lord of the Towne': Urban Identity and Culture in Late Tudor and Stuart Stockport' *Transactions of the Historic Society of Lancashire and Cheshire* 148, 27-58.

Phillips C B & Smith J H (eds) 1985 *Stockport Probate Records 1578-1619*, Record Society of Lancashire and Cheshire 124.

Phillips C B & Smith J H (eds) 1992 *Stockport Probate Records 1620-1650*, Record Society of Lancashire and Cheshire 131.

Porter R E 1976 'The Marketing of Agricultural Produce in Cheshire during the 19th Century' *Transactions of the Historic Society of Lancashire and Cheshire* 126, 139-55.

Radcliffe W 1828 *Origin of the New System of Manufacture Commonly Called Power-loom Weaving*, Stockport (reprinted 1974, Clifton New Jersey, Augustus M Kelley Publishers).

RCHME 1993 *30a (Staircase Cafe) and 31, Market Place, Stockport, Manchester - Historic Building Report*, Royal Commission on the Historical Monuments of England.

Reid C A N 1974 *The Chartist Movement in Stockport*, unpublished MA thesis, University of Hull.

Richards R 1947 *Old Cheshire Churches*, London, B T Batsford.

Robinson B R 1977 *Aviation in Manchester: A Short History*, The Manchester Branch of the Royal Aeronautical Society.

Robinson J M 1979 *The Wyatts: An architectural dynasty*, Oxford University Press.

Schmiechen J & Carls K 1999 *The British Market Hall: A Social and Architectural History*, Yale University Press.

Smith A 1990 *Fearless, Dauntless, Ne'er Afraid: A History of Stockport Fire Brigade*, Stockport Libraries.

Smith C 1938 *Stockport in the Age of Reform*, 1822-1870, unpublished typescript, SLHL.

Smith W J 1977 'The Staircase Cafe, Stockport: An Interim Report' *Transactions of the Lancashire and Cheshire Antiquarian Society* 79, 14-20.

Stewart-Brown R (ed) 1916 *Lancashire and Cheshire Cases in the Court of Star Chamber, Part I*, Record Society of Lancashire and Cheshire 71.

Stewart-Brown R (ed) 1925 *Calendar of County Court, City Court and Eyre Rolls of Chester, 1259-1297*, Chetham Society, new series, 84.

Stockport County Borough 1945 *Stockport: A Report on Planning and Redevelopment*, Stockport County Borough Planning and Development Committee.

Stockport Express 1946 *Express Annual for 1946*.

Tait J 1904 *Mediaeval Manchester and the Beginnings of Lancashire*, Manchester University Press (reprinted 1991, Llanerch Publishers).

Taylor W M P 1974 *A History of Stockport Court Leet*, revised edition, Stockport Museum Publication No 3, Stockport Library Museum and Art Gallery Service.

Thorp J 1940 *A History of Local Government in Stockport between 1760 and 1820*, unpublished MA thesis, University of Manchester.

Tindall A 1985 'Stockport: the Development of the Town' *Greater Manchester Archaeological Journal* 1, 69-73.

Tupling G H 1945-6 'Lancashire Markets in the Sixteenth and Seventeenth Centuries' *Transactions of the Lancashire and Cheshire Antiquarian Society* 58, 1-34.

Wardle M & Bentham 1814 *The Commercial Directory for 1814-15*, Manchester.

Watkin W T 1886 *Roman Cheshire: a Description of Roman remains in the County of Chester*, Liverpool (reprinted 1974, Wakefield, E P Publishing).

Watson Revd J 1782 *Memoirs of the Ancient Earls of Warren and Surrey and the Descendants to the Present Time*, 2 vols, Warrington.

Wild W I 1896 'Stockport Cross' *Cheshire Notes and Queries*, new series, 1, 77.

Appendix: Occupants of the Market Place, 1825-1910

The following details of the businesses of the occupants of the Market Place are derived principally from trade directories, supplemented by evidence from Land Tax assessments, rate books, census returns and the *Stockport Advertiser*. They also take into account the renumbering of properties in the nineteenth century. In some cases a property was vacant or the occupant has not been identified.

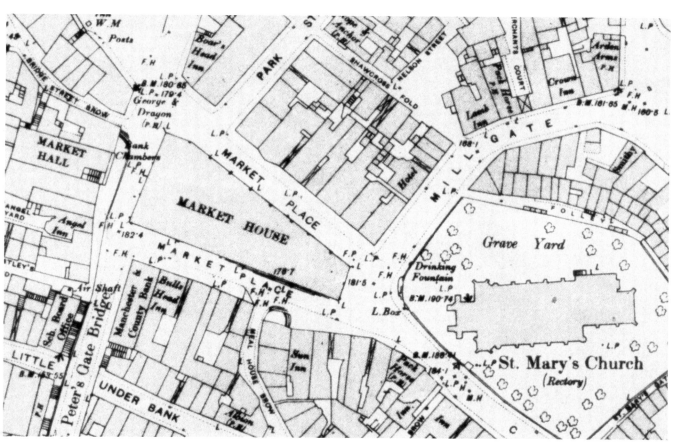

Above: The Market Place on Ordnance Survey mapping of 1893

	1	2	3	4	5	6	7	8
1825	Corn Dealer	Pack Horse	Rose & Crown	Draper	Butcher	Draper	Sun Inn	Ironmonger
1834								
1841								
1850	Eating House		Grocer					
1860					Hatter (Ward)			
1872								
1883				Boot & Shoe Maker		Eating House		
1891								Cheese Dealer
1902	Wines & Spirits							
1910	Bookbinder							

	9	10	11	12	13	14	15	16	17
1825	Hatter	Iron-monger		Draper	Bull's Head	Grocer	Corn Dealer	Grocer?	
1834	Grocer / Brush Maker		Grocer			Grocer			
1841	Hatter		Boot & Shoe Mkr (Wild)			Tea Dealer		Grocer	Chemist
1850	Ironmonger		Soap Maker	Hatter		Grocer	Tea Dealer		Tea & Coffee Dealer
1860						Milliner	Grocer	Clock Maker	Attorney
1872				Tobacco-nist		Bank			
1883									
1891									
1902	Blind Maker	Eating House	Butcher						
1910	Greengrocer's Storeroom								

The properties were demolished in the 1860s for the construction of St Petersgate Bridge.

	18 & 19	20	21	22	23 & 24		25
1825	Furniture Dealer	Angel Inn		Draper	Toll Collector	Post Office	Draper
1834			Tea & Coffee Dealer	(Rostron)			
1841						Weights & Measures	Bank
1850	Chemist						
1860							
1872					*The buildings were demolished in 1850. The Market Hall (later known as the Produce Hall) was built on the site in 1851.*		
1883			Grocer				
1891	Butcher		Draper				
1902							
1910							

26   27

Year					
1825		Draper	Castle Inn	Boar's Head	Grocer?	Chemist
1834	George & Dragon (later Baker's Vaults)				Hatter?	
1841					Draper	
1850		Clock Maker / Draper			Grocer	
1860		The property was demolished in 1861, when the adjoining property (the Baker's Vaults) was rebuilt.	The Castle Inn and Castle Mill were taken down in 1841 and the site (Castle Yard) was made part of the Market Place.		Basket Maker	
1872					Cheese Dealer & Tobacconist	
1883						
1891						
1902					Tobacconist	
1910						

	28	29	30	31	32 & 33	34	35 & 36
1825	Draper	Grocer	Draper	Grocer & Tallow Chandler	Hosier Draper	Draper	Corn & Cheese Dealer
1834							Corn Dealer Hatter
1841							
1850			Boot & Shoe Maker (Wild)		Draper		Corn & Cheese Dealer
1860		Tea & Coffee Dealer					Grocer
1872							
1883		Grocer		Grocer			
1891	Clothier (Emerson)					Boot & Shoe Maker	
1902						Grocer	
1910		Meat Seller		Eating House			Meat Seller Grocer